The Miracle

Mission

The incredible story of the Miami Rescue
Mission's first 100 years and beyond

Walter Villa

The Miracle Mission

© Copyright 2022, Fig Factor Media, LLC.
All rights reserved.

For more information, contact:

Fig Factor Media, LLC | www.figfactormedia.com
JJR Marketing, Inc. | www.jjrmarketing.com

Cover Design by Marco Álvarez
Layout by Juan Manuel Serna Rosales

Printed in the United States of America

ISBN: 978-1-7342369-0-3
Library of Congress Control Number: 2022916666

I dedicate this to my late father, Roberto, and my amazing mother, Berenice, as well as to Michelle and Valentina, who have changed my life for the better.

Table of Contents

INTRODUCTION

In the summer of 2019, I was assigned to interview Rev. Ronald Brummitt. All I knew at the time was that he served as the CEO of the Miami Rescue Mission.

Once Ron started to tell me about his life, my jaw dropped. His tale was so raw, painful and unflinchingly honest that my first thought was that he didn't quite get that I was a reporter.

"Do you understand," I finally said, "that I am quoting you for publication?"

Ron assured me that he understood and that this was his testimony.

With that bit of business out of the way, I proceeded to apologize.

"Ron," I said, "there is only space for 300 words in this Miami Dade College publication. Your story should really be a book or a movie."

Six months after I had completed that assignment, I got a call from out of the proverbial blue.

"It's Ron Brummitt," he said. "How would you like to write that book?"

That call, as it turns out, was heaven sent. Writing this book has given me a much deeper understanding of homelessness and of the miracles that are happening every day at the Miami Rescue Mission.

Here, then, is that book.

Movie to follow?

-Walter Villa

2022

The Miracle Mission

PART 1

FAITH, COURAGE AND IMPOSSIBILITIES

How The Miami Rescue Mission Came To Be

Reverend Ronald Brummitt

From homelessness to CEO/President of the Miami Rescue Mission, here is the story of Reverend Ronald Brummitt's improbable road to redemption

His mother's face, bloodied and disfigured ... Kitchen knives used as weapons ... Two alcoholic parents ...

This is what Ronald Brummitt–while still in grade school got used to seeing in his home.

Born in Richmond, Virginia, on October 23, 1954, Brummitt lived at first on an old farm with no running water or plumbing. In fact, there were no electrical appliances at all. There was an old wood stove, and water was pumped into the kitchen.

If you needed the bathroom at night, you used a pot. During the day, there was an outhouse.

Brummitt was just a boy, but he remembered getting up early every day to feed the chickens.

"I thought that farm was the best thing in the world," Brummitt said. "It wasn't until later that I figured out we weren't well off."

When he was five, his parents moved part of the family–

which included Ron and an older sister – to Miami. Three of their brothers were left behind with family members.

Brummitt didn't know it at that time, but his parents were alcoholics. They moved around a lot because his father– who worked as a pest-control technician– had been married previously and was, in essence, trying to skip out on alimony and child-support payments owed to his ex-wife and their three children.

Brummitt said he witnessed his parents fighting and squabbling often. There were obvious grounds for charges of domestic violence and child abuse. But, in the 1960s, those terms weren't discussed, at least not in his family.

"I would come home from school, and here's my mom. She's laying behind the couch, so bloodied, so purple and so disfigured that you can't even tell it's a human face," Brummitt said. "My dad, when he got drunk, he would abuse us, hurt us. I still have scars today where he knifed me.

"He was such a nice guy when he wasn't drinking."

Brummitt said his father had at least those eight children, maybe more. In fact, Brummitt was one of two sons his dad had who were both born in 1954, each from a different mother. (Brummitt has met that half-brother just once in his life.)

Things got so bad for Brummitt's parents that they gave their three youngest children up for adoption, including two who were taken in by Brummitt's maternal grandparents. The third was adopted by another family.

Brummitt said his mother, while abused by his dad, was no innocent victim. She would throw knives.

"My dad would reach his breaking point, and then it was over," Brummitt said. "He'd lash out."

Brummitt, who received no monetary allowance from his parents, was resourceful as a youngster – the same resourcefulness he would later demonstrate as the head of the Miami Rescue Mission. He started a lawn-cutting service when he was about 12, hiring boys in the neighborhood.

"I was making some pretty good money, but I couldn't keep it because my mom would steal it," Brummitt said. "I had to hide it, but she was very aggressive. She liked knives."

When Brummitt would come home after making money with his lawn service, he would make a bee-line for his bedroom, closing the door behind him as fast as possible.

His mother, inevitably drunk, would give chase.

"She needed money. She wanted a beer, whatever. She wanted something," Brummitt said. "I'd lock the door, but I put my shoulder against it so she couldn't come in. She's smart. She's got the knife. She's putting her knife underneath the door. She would slide her knife back and forth to get me to move so she could bust in – it was just horrible."

Brummitt rarely heard the words "I love you" from his parents, and the same was true for his siblings.

"We were just tolerated," he said. "I think we were a constant reminder of their botched past, and I ended up with, unfortunately, a very unhealthy hatred for my parents.

"I would pray for their demise. I would yell at them, 'I hope you die, and I will spit on your grave'."

Brummitt yearned for love, approval, acceptance.

"It was a love-hate relationship because they're still your parents," he said. "You want to feel loved by them, but you don't have anything to really judge on until you start going to other people's non-dysfunctional homes. That's when the lights went on because I said, 'Wait a second now'."

Growing up, Brummitt feared the holidays.

"There would be drinking -- food would be burned, things would be thrown around," Brummitt said. "People would get upset, Christmas trees would be destroyed.

"The morning may have started off really well, but, by one o'clock, two o'clock in the afternoon, it was a disaster."

When Brummitt was 10, his mother nearly died when she wrecked her Volkswagen Beetle. Her face was disfigured due to major scars suffered in the crash.

"She was very attractive when she was young," Brummitt said. "But now she's not attractive, which did not help her self-esteem.

"Later in life, I saw pictures of that VW, and it's amazing she came out alive. But she survived, and now she started drinking even more because of her face and the guilt of leaving kids behind."

What he witnessed in his house was so depraved that Brummitt promised himself he would never drink. He would be the best parent in the world. He would never replicate his parents' mistakes. But addiction and abuse can often be cyclical, a sad hand-me-down from parent to child, as Brummitt would later discover.

A KNOCK AT THE DOOR

Although Brummitt's life has taken many twists, he feels fortunate that – one fateful day – a man of the cloth came knocking on his door.

His name was Pastor Arnold Warner, and he was going door to door to see if the residents of the Village Green section of southwest Miami were interested in attending his Sunday services.

Brummitt, who was about 10 at the time, started going to church with his sister. Their parents were only too happy to have the kids out of the house for a couple of hours.

"That was a turning point in my life," Brummitt said. "I believed in Jesus Christ, but I hadn't gone to church in a long time. Pastor Warner would come pick us up, and that really started something special that has lasted a lifetime. I accepted Jesus Christ as my Savior at that church and began to learn scripture verses. I became close to the pastor and his family. Even though Pastor Warner has since passed away, I still remain close to his family."

Brummitt said the pastor took a special interest in him and his sister due to their family circumstances. The pastor would arrive at the door and see Brummitt's parents drunk, and it didn't take a genius to figure out that these two children needed help.

For Brummitt, church was a setting where he was finally free of stress, if only for an hour.

"I felt welcomed. I felt loved," he said. "Those were things I didn't feel at home. Besides learning scripture, this became like a surrogate family for me. It was a better family."

Brummitt was a straight-A student in those days.

Still looking for his parents' approval, he was also a talented musician and athlete.

None of that mattered to his mom and dad, however. They never came to any of his baseball games. They never saw him play guitar or trumpet in his high school's band.

Brummitt was so talented that he was offered a music scholarship to attend the University of Miami. He was going to be the trumpet player in their jazz band, except that there was just one problem:

UM was too close to home.

Too close to his parents.

Too close to the misery he wanted so badly to escape.

Brummitt got his chance to flee when recruiters from the U.S. Army came to his high school, Miami Southwest, and played a tape of their military band.

"The recruiters said I could join the service and be in this wonderful band," Brummitt said. "I thought, 'Oh my goodness, this is fantastic. I can be a musician and serve my country'."

That's how Brummitt was transformed from a self-described "geeky" high school kid who was into comic books and had never done drugs … into a private in the U.S. Army.

Once he got out of basic training, however, he found out that the promise of this "fantastic" band was a straight-up lie.

"It was a con job," Brummitt said.

What actually happened was that Brummitt would be the

bugler who would play "Taps" at military funerals. The "Taps" tradition in the U.S. Army goes back to 1874, and Brummitt got really good at the song because he played it nearly every weekend for two years.

This was during the final months of the Vietnam War, and the body count was high.

RACISM AND INJUSTICE

Brummitt would travel around to Alabama, Georgia and other southern states for military funerals, and what he witnessed wounded him inside. He saw racism for the first time as some in Brummitt's traveling party were Black officers, and the treatment they received was appalling.

Aside from that harsh reality, life on the road and in the military was a lonely existence. All he had ever wanted was to feel like he belonged –somewhere by someone.

To fit in, Brummitt did something outside of what had been his character up to that time.

"I was considered an outcast in high school because I wasn't going to get involved in drinking and drugs," Brummitt said. "But when I got in the service, I felt I was becoming a man. Drinks were cheap at the servicemen's club, so I started with orange juice and vodka, and I liked it.

"It took away all the pain of my past. I just put that aside. This was a new chapter, new road, new destiny."

Brummitt eventually started smoking marijuana … and then dealing pot, too.

From there, Brummitt started taking pills and dropping acid, also known as LSD.

As badly as he didn't want to become his parents, it was happening, and now his genetic predisposition to addiction took hold.

Once, after taking LSD, Brummitt went to buy drugs from a military cook who went by the name "Red."

Brummitt knocked on the door.

No answer.

Brummitt saw Red's car parked out front. Already high on drugs, Brummitt started banging on trash cans to get Red's attention.

Finally, the door flew open, and Red pointed a .357 chrome-plated Smith & Wesson revolver at Brummitt's head.

"Do you know how close you came to me blowing your head off?" Red said after he put the gun down.

Brummitt, who was 17 when he joined the Army, lasted three years in the service. That near-death encounter with Red's gun should have been the end of his drug days.

But it wasn't.

A DANGEROUS OCCUPATION

When he got out of the service in 1975, he had a lot of connections with members of the military who returned home with large quantities of hashish, which is made from the resin of the cannabis plant.

"Since they were servicemen, they weren't being checked in

those days at the airport," Brummitt said. "So, I got into the hash business, and that led to me finding out about cocaine.

"Now, cocaine in the mid-1970s was what all the musicians, actresses and actors were doing. It was for the elite.

"I remember going to a place like the Jockey Club in Miami and passing around plates of cocaine, seeing all the stars at the time. And I started moving up the chain pretty fast as far as who I was associated with and the quantity of what I was selling."

Brummitt became more and more brazen about his illegal activity.

In 1977, he left a friend's house in a stolen car. There was also a gun in the car that Brummitt didn't even know the origins of or how it got there.

In addition, Brummitt had five pounds of pot and an ounce of cocaine in the trunk. He had Quaaludes stuffed in his shirt, and he had all sorts of scales and other instruments to weigh and cut the drugs.

If that weren't bad enough, Brummitt was driving while severely impaired.

"I was higher than a kite, and I ran off the road off of 8th Street and SW 127 Avenue," he said. "I hit a light pole."

Once the police arrived, they saw the pills, and they had probable cause to break open the trunk, where they discovered the drugs.

"If you had even a gram of cocaine back at that time, you were looking at 20 years," Brummitt said. "So, they throw me in jail. A few hours later, here came these two hippy-dippy-looking guys with full beards.

"They said, 'We got you. You're going away for a long time.' And they were just gloating over me and just laughing it up, talking among themselves. saying: 'He won't be out before he's 60.'

"At this point, I'm not high any longer. Reality has kicked in, and I'm pooping in my pants.

"Stolen car, unregistered weapon, cocaine,

pot, evidence of dealing because it was obvious with all the instruments I had that this wasn't for personal use."

The two hippy-dippy undercover cops offered Brummitt a deal: Become an informant to bring down other drug dealers … or go to jail.

"They wanted me to be a rat fink," Brummitt said. "They wanted me to rat out everybody."

That wasn't something Brummitt wanted to do, but …

"I looked at the people that I was hanging out with, and one guy was an escaped con from Atlanta. Another guy, he was a rip-off guy. The other guy was a bondsman who had lost his mind and was shooting people," Brummitt said. "I thought, 'I don't owe these people anything.' So, I became an informant."

These were the days of the so-called Cocaine Cowboys, and Colombian drug cartels were moving their product to Miami and New York.

Undercover cops tried to stop them, but Brummitt could tell that the officers who came to talk to him were new at the game.

"This was not Miami Vice," Brummitt said. "These guys

didn't really know what they were doing. It was pretty obvious.

"Meanwhile, I would take cocaine on a flight to New York. I would meet people in New York and sell ounces, which was pretty big to move. If you've got two or three ounces … it's like $1,600 an ounce. And then they would break it down in grams.

"I sold grams. I would step on it, which meant I would mix other chemicals to lower the quality. This was common. It was half cocaine, half crap, but it was still enough to get high."

Brummitt was selling to bondsmen, lawyers – all kinds of people. Calls would come in at 3 a.m. sometimes. He was still doing business even though he was supposed to be acting as an informant.

"I was acting as if the dope I was selling the DEA was from another dealer, but it wasn't," he said. "It was from me.

"One time, I had just gotten my cocaine. I was taking the bus home, and I had the drugs in a brown paper bag. I get to my apartment, and, lo and behold, here they are."

It was a surprise visit from the DEA's undercover cops, looking to make a drug bust.

"I'm crapping in my pants because I had an ounce of coke in that bag," Brummitt said. "I was going to eventually get the other guy I was doing my little scam with (busted). I was doing a double-sided thing. How stupid could I be?

"So, the DEA guys said, 'We're going to have to just check you out before we let you in the house to make sure that you're not carrying anything in there.'

"I put down my paper bag down. They frisked me all over, and they said, 'He's clean.' I then picked up my paper bag and walked into the place. They never checked my bag! Oh my, Lord Jesus."

After that, the sting was on – the undercover cops were going to buy cocaine from Brummitt's associates for $10,000 and then make arrests.

The only problem was that Brummitt's associates were planning a rip-off, and a shoot-out was looking like the end result. Brummitt knew it was to be a rip-off because he heard his associates making their plans, not knowing, of course, that they were dealing with undercover cops.

"I'm thinking, 'This is going to be a bloodbath tonight'," Brummitt said. "I saw that as my way out. I said, 'Look, I'm not part of this, guys. I'm out.'"

Brummitt went back outside and was able to tip the DEA cops about the planned rip-off, scribbling a quick note on a piece of paper.

The cops then made their arrests, including Brummitt in an effort to show he was not an informant.

Brummitt, fearing for his life from his fellow drug dealers as revenge for the set-up, moved to the Orlando area, where he had an aunt. He started working construction, but he was still smoking pot.

"You would think that after all that I would never do drugs or alcohol again, but that's the insanity of addiction," Brummitt said.

"People want to have wine with dinner – I'm not against it for people who can keep it under control. But, because of my addictive behavior and the damage it has done in my life, I hate it like crazy."

After two years spent in the Central Florida city of Lakeland, Brummitt – who was drinking heavily and smoking pot but still yearning for harder drugs – decided to move back to Miami. He had lost his job in Lakeland, he was behind in his rent payments, and the Magic City beckoned.

SEARCHING FOR PURPOSE

This was in 1979, and Brummitt moved back in with his parents in what to him felt like a tale from *The Twilight Zone*.

"I remember the episode about the man who woke up and didn't remember his past, but he was in jail," Brummitt said. "I felt like that was me – I was in kind of a jail, but I didn't know exactly how I got there. I felt defeated. I felt I had no purpose in life.

"So, I called my old pastor (Arnold Warner). I needed to get my life back with the Lord."

Pastor Warner told Brummitt that he wouldn't do well living with his parents – too many bad influences.

Instead, Brummitt moved in with Warner and started studying the Bible. Equipped with a positive and stable home life, Brummitt got a job in construction and met a woman at church that he liked.

"Kelly was the complete opposite of me," Brummitt said. "She had never done drugs.

"We fell in love."

The couple got married in August of 1980. It was a small church wedding that went off the rails when Brummitt's mother got drunk and said more than a few nasty things.

Still, the honeymoon period was relatively blissful. They moved to Lakeland, and Kelly got a job at Burger King. Brummitt was at Bible College, studying to be a preacher while also working at a hardware store.

Then Kelly got pregnant.

"That news was the joy of my life," Brummitt said. "I promised the Lord I was going to be a great dad and give my son a great home."

Sadly, Brummitt was still getting drunk at night and managing to hide it from Kelly.

About three years into their marriage, Brummitt finally admitted to Kelly that he had a drinking problem. But it was too late. Fed up with the drinking and the lies, Kelly and their son, Roger – who was six months old at the time – moved out and went to live with her parents back in Miami.

Brummitt stayed in Lakeland and earned his degree in theology. He moved back to Miami, with his parents, got a job at McDonald's, quickly working his way up to store manager. He was also taking computer-science classes, but Kelly wouldn't let him see Roger.

"I had a theology degree, but how could I tell anybody what to do?" Brummitt said. "I was a drunk."

Again, he tasted the sourness of rejection. Disappointing others was a natural trigger to the painful path he now walked.

Pretty soon, it got worse. Brummitt started using cocaine, and Kelly filed for divorce. Brummitt fought it, but the legal motions went against him, and the divorce was finalized in 1985.

SEVEN LOST YEARS

From the time Kelly moved out in 1983 until 1990 – those were seven lost years for Brummitt. He lost his job at McDonald's and got a telemarketing job that he knew was a scam.

He then committed his most grave error yet – getting involved with crack cocaine from 1987 to 1989.

"That was my last downfall," Brummitt said. "Crack took all my willpower, energy and personhood."

When his mother died in 1988, tons of people came out to the services to console Brummitt, but it did no good.

"I was in the slavery of drug addiction," Brummitt said. "Drugs were all I wanted to do."

After she died, Brummitt's father moved to Virginia. Brummitt was able to sell drugs, but he spent his profits on crack, and he became homeless, sleeping on the street, between a restaurant and an office building.

Brummitt would spend his days begging for food at a convenience store, resting at a public library or park.

After Kelly remarried, he lost contact with her, and he had no means with which to pay child support.

"I was a deadbeat dad," Brummitt said.

"People see the homeless, and they say, 'Go get a job.'

"But they don't know the whole story. It's not that easy. You have an addiction or a mental illness – or both. It's not easy. You don't have a solid place to put your feet.

"Many times, the homeless turn to drugs not to get high but just so that they don't feel any more pain, and I can testify from personal experience."

Brummitt said he often contemplated suicide, plotting the chosen method in his mind. He considered jumping in front of a speeding bus or drowning himself by using a weight or anchor.

For a while, he would venture to a crack house in downtown Miami, which was very nearly suicidal in and of itself.

"I was the only white guy there," Brummitt said. "They called me the 'crazy white guy', but I was fearless. I didn't care if I got knifed or beat up, and there were many times that I was robbed at gunpoint. They took what little money I had – five people going through my pockets."

Brummitt reached proverbial rock bottom in December of 1989 on an unusually yet brutally cold Miami night.

Dressed in typical Miami garb – sandals, shorts and a T-shirt – Brummitt was totally unprepared for this cold front. Homeless, he was sleeping in an alley across the street from a bank that had a large digital billboard with the current temperature.

Brummitt remembers the mercury hitting 50 … and then 40 … and then 30 …. and then the high 20s.

With no blanket and no money for even a cheap hotel room, Brummitt used a cardboard box to try to keep warm.

"I finally went into the neighborhood, knocking on doors, looking for a blanket," Brummitt said. "It's almost Christmas, but nobody would answer the door."

THE LAST PHONE CALL

The next night, when the frigid temperature returned, Brummitt found a payphone and made an angry collect call to his pastor.

"I'm lashing out," Brummitt said. "I told him, 'I hope you have a great Christmas because I'm out here freezing.'

"But instead of hanging up, he said, 'Son, where are you? I will come and get you.'"

Pastor Warner tried to take Brummitt to the Miami Rescue Mission. But Brummitt was not yet ready for that step in his life. He was cold and hungry but not ready to submit to a program with all its rules, even though that was precisely what was needed to transform his life.

Instead of the mission, Warner took Brummitt to his house in South Miami, offering him a room in an incredible act of kindness.

But Brummitt didn't want that, either.

"I felt subhuman at that time," Brummitt said. "I didn't feel comfortable sleeping in his house. Here was a man (Pastor Warner) and his family who had helped me, and all I had ever done was disappoint them.

"So, I asked him for a couple of blankets, and I slept in his yard, under a tree. They gave me some food, but all the memories of being married and my son, Roger, and what could've been came crashing down on me. I couldn't go into his home. I had no self-esteem."

The next day, Brummitt – out of options at this point – went to the mission.

"I didn't want to be hungry anymore, and this was a Christian organization, which was and is dear to my heart," Brummitt said.

"I was crying out to the Lord. 'God, you love me, and you've given me opportunities, but all I do is spit in your face. I ruined not only my life but also Kelly's life and Roger's life'. I didn't feel worthy of the Lord."

Once Brummitt got to the mission, he liked that it was warm. He was well fed, and he had clean clothes.

But all of that came with rules required to stay in the program, and that included being free of drugs, which wasn't going to be easy for Brummitt.

"I still had that monster on my back," Brummitt said. "I still wanted to do drugs."

At first, Brummitt was in a dorm room with about 25 other men, and virtually all of them were also addicted to crack. The men had to be drug-free for eight months to be considered a graduate and ready to find a job.

There was also daily chapel service, and, pretty soon, Brummitt became determined to stay at the mission.

"I was in chapel one day, and I bowed my head and started weeping," Brummitt said. "I said, 'Lord, I have said this to you before. I have called out to you and pleaded. But today I'm surrendering. Every part of my body is yours. Can you use me in some way? Can you heal me in some way?'

"I took an imaginary white flag and laid it down at the altar."

But, despite Brummitt's best intentions, a petty argument with one of his fellow recovering addicts nearly pushed him back to the streets.

"I was angry, and I said, 'This ain't no Christian place.' I grabbed my bag of clothes, and I decided to leave."

Brummitt walked down from the fourth floor, defeated. But just as he was about to exit the building, he saw a distinguished-looking man in a gray suit. Brummitt didn't know it at the time, but that was Dr. Franklin Jacobs, who ran the mission and was a person who would become incredibly influential in his life.

"Dr. Jacobs saw me leaving and said, 'Son, where are you going'?" Brummitt recalled. "I said, 'Who are you? What business is it of yours?'"

Just then, Jacobs, a man of God, placed his hand on Brummitt's shoulder and said, "Son don't leave this place. You don't know what God has for you here."

Only the Lord knows what would've happened if Jacobs hadn't intervened at just that moment. Brummitt stayed in the program, pouring all his energy into reading his Bible and helping others at the mission.

Brummitt had been at the mission for just over four months when he spotted an old trumpet at the Mission's Bargain Barn thrift store. Allowed to borrow the trumpet, Brummitt – a talented musician from his younger days – started to practice his instrument.

One day, Jacobs – a terrific tenor singer –overheard Brummitt playing the trumpet. That led to a new partnership.

They would go out into the community to raise money for the mission. Jacobs would preach, and Brummitt would play the trumpet and then share his testimony.

The mission also had a small band that Brummitt joined, providing good cheer for people incarcerated or in hospitals.

All of this community work brought Brummitt and Jacobs closer together.

"Jacobs would pick me up for the events, and we got to know each other," Brummitt said. "He would take me to his house for dinner. Who gets to go to the home of the president of the mission?

"He was the face of the mission, and his wife was the chief of operations in charge of all the administrative stuff. We became close."

By the fall of 1990, Brummitt – clean and sober – had graduated from the mission program. Brummitt's childhood church headed by Pastor Warner decided to build a new building. Brummitt, who had a background in construction, was hired as a laborer.

Rising at 5 a.m., Brummitt would work construction until 2 p.m. and then go back to the mission and teach Bible studies until 11 pm.

Every dollar he made was sent to Kelly and Roger to pay the thousands he owed in child support.

Brummitt said he could hardly believe he was the same person as he had been prior to coming to the mission.

"The life I had lived earlier -- feeling worthless and helpless and lost, begging for food, doing crack and sleeping on the street,"

Brummitt said. "Now I was involved in a band. I had a job. I was paying child support …"

Brummitt was feeling good, and he was constantly telling his band mates about Roger and his hopes of seeing him for Christmas.

One night at a band get-together, Brummitt was put on the spot by one of his friends. Why not call Kelly and ask to see Roger?

"Roger was eight years old at the time," Brummitt said. "I hadn't seen him in four years. I called Kelly about being allowed to see him, and she said: 'That's not going to happen. Roger hates you and never wants to see you again'."

Brummitt played the rejection off in front of his friends, but once he got back to his dorm room, he fell apart.

"I couldn't hold the tears back," he said. "I wanted to quit. I started talking to God. I said, 'Lord, I give up. I'm beat. I tried my best. I turned my life around. I'm a chaplain. I'm a counselor. And yet this is how I'm being treated, and I can't see my son."

Brummitt said he then heard a voice in his head that was outside his normal pattern of thinking:

"Ron, have you done these things because you love me or because you want something from me?"

That's when a realization came to Brummitt.

"I had surrendered my life to the Lord," he said. "But I hadn't surrendered Roger's life. So, I said, 'Lord, Roger is your son. You have to take care of him. Please take care of him'."

FINDING THE COURAGE TO ASK: WHAT IF?

By January of 1991, Brummitt was at a crossroads.

He wanted to stay on staff at the mission, but there were no openings. So, he got creative and made a proposal to Jacobs.

"What this place needs is a real Biblical curriculum that will provide spiritual development but also focus on finances and the ability to get a job," Brummitt told Jacobs.

"Our graduates were too often relapsing and going back to drugs.

"I asked Dr. Jacobs: 'Would you consider, on a trial basis, putting me on staff and starting this program?'"

Personally, Brummitt had three goals at the time:

1: Re-establish his relationship with Roger.

2: Build a solid foundation with Christ.

3: Be involved with the ministry, which is what he was seeking to do with his proposal to Jacobs.

"I had written those goals during my first week as part of the program," Brummitt said.

Jacobs, sensing Brummitt's sincerity, gave him the job he had sought, even though it was for low pay.

Brummitt was elated, and he quickly got to work.

In February of 1991, he started the Alpha program, which is still in existence today.

Brummitt was the teacher and counselor of the program back then, and he lived in a tiny room at the mission. He found an old typewriter at the thrift store and used it to craft his lessons.

There were 26 men in the program that first year, and Brummitt was their father figure and disciplinarian. Armed with his degree in Biblical studies, Brummitt could quote scripture, and he sensed that the men looked up to him.

"I think they felt, 'If he can make it, so can I'," Brummitt said.

But as Brummitt got to know the men on a deeper level, he realized that some of their problems ran deep. There was a literacy issue, and there was a lot of mental illness tracing back to childhood trauma or the effects of having served in wars.

"I was not equipped to deal with them," Brummitt said. "I said, 'I've got to go back to school'."

Brummitt did just that, and he got a license that made him a certified addictions professional, passing an eight-month course that was accredited by the state of Florida.

THE POWER OF FORGIVENESS

For years, Brummitt had prayed to see his son Roger while catching up with child-support payments. Faith was his roadmap.

One day, Kelly called Brummitt and said:

"How would you like to take your son on a camping trip?"

Brummitt was shocked, excited and nervous. He asked Kelly if they could meet at church – chosen as a safe space -- and she agreed.

Dressed in his Sunday best, Brummitt arrived at the church, unsure what to expect.

But as soon as Roger saw his father, the boy sprinted in his dad's direction.

"He jumped onto my chest and put his arms around my neck," Brummitt said. "I said, 'Son, I've missed you so much.'"

"Kelly was dumbfounded looking at us. As it turned out, what Kelly had told me about Roger never wanting to see me was not entirely accurate."

After that meeting, Brummitt started picking Roger up every Saturday. Brummitt at times would miss a meeting when the car he had bought from the thrift store – "a clunker," he called it – broke down.

But even with those issues, Brummitt had begun the hard work of repairing the damage done to his relationship with his son.

In addition, Brummitt, who had been estranged from his own father, tried to mend that fence as well.

"He had been writing me letters," Brummitt said. "He was no longer drinking. We were encouraging each other. I told him, 'Why don't you come stay with me?'"

"So, he stayed in my little room at the mission. One day, we took a road trip to Virginia, where we had family.

"My dad had been an alcoholic and abusive. He left me with scars, both physically and mentally, but I had forgiven him.

"So, we were driving. We were up in North Carolina, and, out of the blue, he looked at me and said, 'Son, I need you to forgive me. I know I was a terrible father and husband. Do you ever think you can forgive me?'

"I had tears in my eyes. I grabbed his hand and said, 'Dad, I forgave you a long time ago.'"

MORE WORK TO BE DONE

By 1997, Brummitt was experiencing professional success at the mission and yet emotional upheaval in his private life.

At work, he added an Omega class for graduates of the Alpha program.

"The idea was that we would support our Alpha graduates for six months to help them build their finances and secure housing," Brummitt said.

On the home front, Brummitt's second marriage ended in divorce. It had survived only three years.

Brummitt also learned that year that his son Roger had begun experimenting with drugs.

That was heartbreaking.

Meanwhile, Jacobs made Brummitt the director of the Miami Rescue Mission's Miami Centers.

"There were people more qualified than I was for that position," Brummitt said. "But Dr. Jacobs said, 'Ron, you know this place inside and out,' and he put everything in the building under my responsibility and I then reported directly to Mrs. Maxine Jacobs."

Brummitt soon brought in volunteers to help the men learn to read and write. Brummitt also wanted to open a computer learning center, giving the men a chance to earn their GEDs and possibly go to a trade school.

But the cost for implementing the program was high, and Jacobs told Brummitt there simply wasn't room in the budget to get it done.

Soon after, there were ceremonies for the men who had

graduated the Alpha program. At one of those ceremonies, about 150 people showed up for the celebration.

"At the ceremony, one of the graduates got up to speak and opened his Bible and started reading," Brummitt said, "The graduate said, 'I came here seven months ago, and I could barely read anything. Now, I can read the Bible.'

"I looked over, and I saw Dr. Jacobs had tears in his eyes. The next week, Dr. Jacobs asked me, 'Ron, what would it take to get that computer-learning center started?'"

It took two years, but Brummitt helped open the Jeffrey A. Tew Educational Center, with 25 computer stations. It was named after Tew, one of the longest-standing board members of the mission, who was instrumental in getting the funds for the new Center for Men.

"The men in our program could work at their own pace, but they had to go there for four to eight hours per week and do a complete education analysis. We had volunteer tutors come in, and our goal was to get them to a ninth-grade level. Beyond that, they can also get their GED, and thousands have accomplished that feat," Brummitt said.

"Even today, you can see men and women at our centers, dressed up, going over their lessons so that they can make decisions, get jobs and sign apartment leases."

The Miami Center was revolutionary. In fact, at the time when the mission opened its doors in Broward County – specifically in Hollywood – it was essentially a carbon copy of the Miami Center.

Later, at 2056 Scott Street, the mission opened Broward's first comprehensive center for the homeless.

"Broward initially had a horrendous homeless problem, with a tent city," Brummitt said. "They were getting national media attention due to the problem, and there weren't many agencies that were helping.

"In 1992, we opened in a humble building inside a strip-shopping center – just a place where we could feed people and give out clothes. Later, in 1997, we bought the building on Scott Street.

"Now there are more agencies providing help, but we're unique. We look at the whole person, developing their character through faith. We teach them skills and give them tools so that these men and women have a greater chance to not relapse."

Back in Dade County, Brummitt had become the Miami mission's de facto afternoon chaplain.

Every afternoon, he would invite the homeless and the needy for dinner, and he noticed many of the women were also bringing their children.

"I did magic tricks to entertain the kids," Brummitt said. "One of the boys was interested in how I did the 'disappearing quarter' trick. He wasn't doing that well in school, so I said: 'If you improve your grades, I will show you the trick.'

"All it took was one person to show interest in that child, and the boy quickly improved his grades."

Buoyed by that encounter, Brummitt started thinking about what he and the mission could do to help the growing number of women and children showing up at their door that were hungry.

The need to help at-risk families was increasing as these families were coming to eat the evening meal at the mission. Brummitt realized that these families needed help before they became homeless. He worried about the children that were susceptible to the lure of the streets and drug dealers. As it happened, there was a vacant lot across the street from the mission. It used to be a transmission shop that was torn down, but Brummitt saw it as the answer to his prayers.

"We needed an activity or youth center to give these kids a chance," Brummitt said. "In 1999, I went to Dr. Jacobs and said: 'There's this property …'"

Unfortunately, Jacobs said the funds were simply not there for that type of expansion.

"Don't waste your time," Jacobs told Brummitt.

Undaunted, Brummitt prayed for months, hoping for some sort of miracle. In fact, every Friday, Brummitt and about 15 other homeless residents and co-workers prayed specifically for the youth center. They called it PAY day, which stood for Pray About Youth.

One day, Jacobs happened upon the prayer group, standing in the vacant lot. When Jacobs asked what was happening, Brummitt said: "We're going to keep on praying to see what God can do."

Two months later, Jacobs called Brummitt into his office and said: "Ron, you're not going to believe this, but a man I've never met before told me he's dying and that God wanted him to do something for kids."

That man then proceeded to write a check for $1 million, which proved to be the catalyst for the purchase of the very land they were praying on and later the youth center was built.

"That was a dream come true," Brummitt said. "It's a place where kids can do their homework, play sports, take dance classes and have a safe space to come to."

The Community Activity Center was opened in November of 2001.

This began the after-school program for at-risk children in the neighborhood. Years later through a burden of one of the board members Marty Steinberger, CARE Elementary, which stands for Christian Academy for Reaching Excellence, was started. It serves kindergarten through sixth grade.

LOVE WINS

By 1999, Brummitt – now twice divorced – had decided he wasn't going to get romantically involved with anyone again. His sole focus was the mission and serving the Lord.

God had a different plan, however.

Marilyn Sharp had been a widow for 11 years when she met Brummitt in 2000. They became acquainted through a mutual friend, and they were just platonic at first.

However, late that year, Marilyn invited Brummitt to a Christmas party, and suddenly, there was the possibility of more than just friendship.

"I touched her hand. She squeezed my hand," Brummitt

said. "I started to get those butterflies. We had a lot in common, and our chemistry clicked."

In February of 2001, the Rev. Harry Gordon asked Brummitt if he would like to go to Israel. Gordon had by then volunteered at the Miami Rescue Mission as a chaplain for 20 years. This trip to Israel had been a life-long dream for Brummitt, but he told Rev. Gordon he didn't have the money for such an expensive trip.

"I didn't ask you if you had the money," Gordon said. "I asked if you wanted to go."

Flabbergasted, Brummitt said yes, and he went to Israel as Gordon's unofficial security detail.

Brummitt by then was already in love with Marilyn, but given his poor history in relationships, he was unsure how to proceed or even if he should proceed.

"I told Marilyn, "I will go to Israel, and I will pray on this," Brummitt said.

In Israel, there had been a spate of recent bombings. Because of that, there were few tourists, and Brummitt found a lot of much-needed solitude.

Brummitt used that time and space to pray, asking the Lord if he should go forward with his blossoming feelings for Marilyn.

When he got back to Miami, Brummitt had made his decision.

"I asked her to marry me, and she said yes," Brummitt said. "We set the date for February of 2002."

Today, both feel their marriage has been blessed and ordained by God. Marilyn is more than just a wife – she is also

Brummitt's ministry partner.

But that doesn't mean there weren't adjustments at first, especially since Marilyn has a daughter and a son from her previous marriage.

"Her daughter was married, and her son Mark had just started college," Brummitt said. "And here I come, Mr. Loser.

"She knew my history. How does a guy like me end up with a wonderful woman like her? And she really loves the Lord."

Marilyn was an accomplished businesswoman before she met Brummitt. She had her own business — two appliance stores – in the 1980s. She was also a mini-celebrity in her area conducting weekly microwave cooking classes, writing a cooking column in the local newspaper and advertising on TV and radio.

But, even so, she may have been a bit naïve when it came to dealing with the homeless, some of whom are adept at manipulating people, Brummitt said.

"She's the complete opposite of me (in terms of naiveté)," Brummitt said. "She was 'green' when she came to the mission. She was taken advantage of at times.

"But she's learned. She has a big heart, but now she knows who is genuine and who isn't."

Everything has worked out, Brummitt said.

"When we got married, one of my hopes was that we could work in the ministry together. She had hoped to work at the center for women and children but the only position open was for a volunteer coordinator in 2002. Marilyn ended up loving that position, which gave her access to all the departments.

"She started connecting the community to the mission and later became the director of development and then the VP of Development. She continued to transform and expand the mission's footprint."

HEARTBREAKING NEWS

While Brummitt found bliss with Marilyn, there has been no greater heartache than his relationship with his son, Roger.

Brummitt's drinking and drug-taking had taken a toll on Roger, even when it wasn't always apparent.

It seemed the relationship became very strong between father and son, and Roger got married in 2004. Pretty soon thereafter, Brummitt became a grandfather to Daniela. Later, two more daughters were born, Sophia and Samantha.

Brummitt sensed that Roger was doing well. But then there were some legal troubles.

"My son and his wife became estranged in 2015," Brummitt said. "He began drinking heavily, and he got involved with drugs, wasting all his money. He already had some mental-health issues."

On Oct. 19, 2015, Brummitt was writing a blog, which was meant to encourage his staff.

In his blog, Brummitt told the story of Marilyn's daughter Joy, who suffered a bloody toe after stepping on a toothpick.

"The message was that, in life, things happen, but God will never forsake you," Brummitt said. "After I finished writing, I got in my truck to go home, and I got a call at 3 p.m. from Roger's wife. She said, 'Ron, I'm so sorry ...'"

As soon as she said that, Brummitt's heart sank. He didn't need to hear the rest.

He knew.

Roger was gone – suicide.

He was just 33.

"I was shell-shocked," Brummitt said. "I had just seen him a few days earlier. What I had written in my blog about God not forsaking you, well that haunted me. I also had a lot of shame and a lot of guilt.

"Roger never got over my absence, and he would bring that up from time to time. He was so close to his three daughters, but he was hurting, and he didn't reach out to me and just decided to kill himself."

Brummitt's birthday, Oct. 23, is also the anniversary of the day he buried his son, and that's a pain that never goes away.

Roger left three suicide notes: one for his mother, one for his wife and one for his daughters.

He didn't leave one for Brummitt, and that still stings as well.

"It's awful enough when you lose someone you love to cancer or a car accident," Brummitt said. "But when that someone hates their life so much and hates their pain so much ... "

THE COURAGE TO APPLY

In May of 2004, Brummitt was reading the NonProfit Times, a magazine geared toward ministry executives.

"I saw this tiny ad in the corner – I still have it," Brummitt said of what has become one of his treasured keepsakes. "The ad said, 'CEO wanted for faith-based organization.'

"It listed a P.O. Box, and it was our mission's P.O. Box."

The next day, Brummitt showed the ad to Jacobs, who told him the board was looking for his successor. The board of directors, Jacobs said, wanted a CEO with fund-raising experience at a big non-profit organization.

"Dr. Jacobs told me, 'I don't want to hurt your feelings, but (the job is for) somebody with more experience in non-profit accounting and fundraising.'"

Jacobs told Brummitt that now that he had seen the advertisement, he should apply.

Brummitt talked it over with Marilyn, who encouraged him.

"I hadn't done budgets for millions of dollars," Brummitt said. "I didn't have experience in donor development and fundraising, but that was Marilyn's strong suit. I knew I had management skills and a degree in psychology, and I knew a lot about the inner workings of the mission plus a passion to help the homeless."

The decision was thus made. Brummitt would throw his proverbial hat in the ring, and he was soon granted an interview by the board.

"Don't get your hopes up," Jacobs cautioned. "Don't run out and buy a new house."

Picking a new CEO would not be up to Jacobs. This was the board's decision, but Jacobs was glad that Brummitt was at least going to get a courtesy interview.

"You've been here 14 years," Jacobs said at the time. "You deserve an interview.

"But we have had 100 applications nationwide. We've had 30 interviews and knocked it down to 10 finalists. We then had five in-person interviews."

Jacobs told Brummitt that a job candidate from Orlando was nearly a lock-in to get the job offer.

Brummitt's heart sank – and not from a selfish standpoint.

It was about the mission and its calling to help the "least, the last and the lost" to find hope through God's love.

"In 1990, when I came to the mission, I made a pledge to the Lord," Brummitt said. "My pledge was to serve the Lord, and I wanted to keep this as a gospel-based rescue mission."

In the wrong hands, the mission's original message would be watered down, Brummitt feared.

"In the interview process, I was told that what I had been doing as the director of the Miami Center was backward," Brummitt said. "I was told I had to get with the times."

Brummitt didn't see it that way, and he knew of a study performed at Florida International University on the impressive effectiveness of faith-based organizations on people with addictions.

"I told Dr. Jacobs, 'Doc, I hope you showed that study to the board," Brummitt said.

When it came time for his interview with the board, Brummitt bought a beauty of a black suit with matching shoes. In 14 years at the mission, he had never made such a purchase, living humbly and often wearing hand-me-down clothes from the thrift store.

But this day was different.

Brummitt and Marilyn prayed before he met the board, and when the time came, it was intense.

For nearly four hours, Brummitt took questions, many of which he really couldn't answer.

Board member: "How would you raise $5 million?"

Brummitt: "I guess I would be on the phone with Dr. Jacobs."

Board member: "What if a big donor wanted to donate, but you would have to water down your gospel in order to accept the gift?"

"Brummitt: "No, I wouldn't take it."

And on it went.

Brummitt felt like he had walked through fire on broken glass, but he must have said or done something right because, after 10 days of waiting, he received word that the board wanted to see him again. This was in July of 2004.

"Lord," Brummitt prayed at the time, "just use me where you need me."

When the day came to see the board again, Brummitt put on that same black suit and headed toward Miami's Marriott Hotel on Brickell Avenue.

Brummitt arrived downtown only to find something missing – the other finalists.

The chairman of the board told Brummitt that they had

conducted a wide search that even extended overseas. But, all along, the right person was right there in the mission – Brummitt.

"They told me, 'Ron, you were the only one not to back away from the Bible. You've lived it (as a homeless person). You have all the capabilities'."

Brummitt raced home to tell Marilyn, who started crying tears of joy. They rejoiced and praised the Lord.

The next month, in August of 2004, a meeting was called for the entire staff at the Miami Center so that Jacobs could make the announcement regarding Brummitt.

During that ceremony, Jacobs put his hand on Brummitt's shoulder just as he had 14 years prior.

"In 1990, I was homeless, and I was about to leave when Dr. Jacobs put his hand on my shoulder and said, 'Son, you don't know what God has in store for you'," Brummitt said. "And in a photo I have from the ceremony announcing me as the CEO, Dr. Jacobs has that same hand on that same shoulder, and now he was blessing me to take over the mission.

Dr. Jacobs and his wife Maxine stayed another couple of years to ease the transition.

SEEKING ANSWERS

After Brummitt was named the CEO in waiting in 2004, Jacobs stuck around for nearly two more years to ease the transition.

In the meantime, Brummitt had to find a replacement for him in his previous role, and he had to learn everything about the two Broward County centers. He had to learn about non-profit accounting and budgeting, fund-raising and all the ins and outs of running a then $16-million organization.

One of Brummitt's initiatives as the new CEO was for the mission to buy multiplex homes that could serve as affordable housing for the graduates of the Miami Center. The graduates could move in for a low fee while still getting monitored, saving money along the way so that they could eventually buy their own homes.

So, in 2009, the mission started buying duplexes or multiplexes for about $70,000 and up. Today, these complexes are worth a half a million or more.

"This continued our vision that No One is Homeless" Brummitt said. "We kept our eyes out for good deals, and today we have between 50 and 70 men, women and children in those properties."

Brummitt said that if graduates have a drug or alcohol relapse, they cannot stay in these homes, but they can instead re-enter the regeneration program for a Beta ("refresher") course.

"Everyone who comes in through our door is like one of our children, and we just love them," Brummitt said.

Another initiative was to create the Miami Rescue Mission Health Clinic, which also opened in 2009 and was built to help those without insurance who have been underserved previously. There are now various clinic sites in the community.

This was a vision of Brummitt many years ago and once again a board director Dr. Pete Gutierrez saw the vision and became the overseeing Doctor.

In addition, the mission started *"Vidas Cambiadas,"* which is Spanish for "Changed Lives".

This program was created to help the homeless who are not functional in English. *Vidas Cambiadas* is yet another sign that the mission makes adjustments for the population in an effort to serve its community.

As for the Miami Center, space had become an issue by 2010. That led Brummitt to want to purchase the building next door, which had been converted into a music studio.

One day, Brummitt noticed that the building was for sale. The asking price was $1.1 million.

"We could turn that into an extension of our men's center," Brummitt said. "It would be safer for everyone, a better environment. I found out that the kids who were using it as a music studio didn't want to sell. But their mother was a donor to the Miami Mission, and when she found out that we wanted it, the sale closed in March of 2011 for $1.1 million."

The building had a cement wall splitting the building into two units of 5,000 feet each.

"I figured we could put several dorm rooms in one half, fitting about 78 men," Brummitt said. "In the other half, we could have a large meeting room and extra offices."

Brummitt hired an architect to design what he wanted done with the building. Brummitt also contacted a construction company – run by Michael Capponi, a friend of the mission.

All Brummitt needed now was the money.

Then, after a lot of praying, a special courier dropped off

an envelope – which was totally unexpected. That envelope contained a cashier's check for $600,000 from an estate.

Twenty minutes later, another envelope arrived.

"My hands were shaking," Brummitt said. "I thought maybe it was a letter rescinding the $600,000 gift.

"But when I opened the envelope, it was another gift from another donor, this time for $500,000.

"I started weeping and dancing through the hallways. I'm praising the Lord. I had to sit down because my hands were shaking. 'Thank you, Lord! Thank you, Lord!'

"In 20 minutes, every penny that we invested in the building had been paid in full, from two different donors.

"I took it as God saying, 'Ron, you are doing the right thing.' I believe God is pleased with our ministry."

That building, which opened in 2013, now houses 78 men in three dorms. There's also a conference multi-purpose room that hosts events for the staff and donors.

"It's a beautiful complex," Brummitt said. "God has used Dr. Jacobs so mightily. I just want to build on Dr. Jacobs' accomplishments and take this ministry to another level so that we can help more people."

Today, the Miami Rescue Mission continues to believe in the miracle of ministry

"The key," Brummitt said, "is listening to what the Lord asks so that more people might be served."

The Schleucher and Ash Families

For a century and beyond, the Miami Rescue Mission has answered the poignant need to help those less fortunate

The Miami Rescue Mission – even though it wasn't called that at the time – dates all the way back to 1922.

As chronicled by Suzanne Jones (granddaughter of the Schluechers) in South Florida History Magazine, the husband-and-wife team of John and Zada Schleucher moved from Chicago to Miami in 1918.

Back in Chicago, the couple had enrolled in the Moody Bible Institute, which is where they got interested in mission ork and also had volunteered at Pacific Gardens Mission in Chicago which had been started in 1877. John finished the course and was ordained.

John, whose full-time job was with the South Atlantic Telephone Company, transferred his position to Miami, which is where he and Zada raised their four children: Glenn, Bettye, Jane and Peggy.

But even while raising their young family, the thought of doing mission work was never far from the minds and hearts of

John and Zada. In fact, caring for those less fortunate became one of the main passions of their lives.

For John and Zada, mission work was a spiritual calling, and awareness of homelessness was starting to take root in American life, ever since the publication in 1890 of a book by Jacob Riis called: How The Other Half Lives.

At that time, people dealing with homelessness lived mostly in large, urban areas such as New York City. But the problem was spreading.

Meanwhile, after initially looking at Fort Lauderdale as a potential new home, John and Zada deemed that city too desolate, which it was back in those days. Instead, in 1922, they settled in Miami, where they founded the Grace Mission, located at 19 SW 8 Street.

Miami was no metropolis, either, as the population in 1920 was estimated at just 29,571 souls. But the city was growing, and so was its homeless population and those in dire need of care and assistance.

Initially, the Grace Mission held its nightly meetings in a tent.

Separately, a group of local church-going women started an organization in the late 1920s that was called "Gospel Mission".

Pretty soon after that, the Schleuchers and the Gospel Mission decided to merge. As part of their arrangement, John and Zada operated the mission, and the women served as their advisory board.

In August of 1929 – just two months before the tragic "Wall

Street Crash of 1929" – the mission moved to 538 North Miami Avenue. By then, it was called the Miami City Mission.

THE GREAT DEPRESSION

The collapse of the stock market in 1929 brought on the Great Depression, which created more challenges for the Mission. Bank closings were at an all-time high, leaving local charitable organizations without funds. Prior to 1929 was the Great Miami Hurricane of 1926, which had devastated the Greater Miami area as well. This all happened in the same decade of the 20's.

By 1930, Miami's population had grown to 110,637, according to the census, and a significant portion of those folks were hurting – either homeless or food deprived ... or both. Unemployment rates had risen to an astonishing 25 percent by 1933.

Through those tough times, the mission stood tall. A headline in the now-defunct Miami News praised the mission for caring for 1,226 persons daily. Another newspaper story reported that the mission was supporting 248 families with food and clothing during one month in 1930.

But, as the winter of 1930 approached, an increasing number of men moved to Miami, in part to avoid the crippling cold up north.

At the mission, where they had 190 beds at the time, space for new arrivals was scarce. Food was running low, too, and the crowds at the mission's evening services were growing.

According to another headline, the mission was the "center

of Miami's welfare work." Local churches that supported the mission during this period included Riverside Baptist and Trinity Methodist.

In 1935, the mission's name was changed again. The issue was that the name "Miami City Mission" led people to believe that the mission's vital work was supported by city funds and not reliant on donations.

BECOMING THE MIAMI RESCUE MISSION

As a remedy, the board approved the name change to its current form, Miami Rescue Mission.

By 1940, Miami's population had grown to an estimated 172,000. The mission was growing, too. A Miami Herald story called the mission the city's fastest growing independent charitable organization.

At that point, roughly 400 homeless men were sleeping at the mission. The mission was also feeding about 5,000 men, women and children on a daily basis.

But, in 1941, when World War II started, the economy picked up throughout the U.S. Rent prices also soared, and the mission struggled to come up with the funds to pay its bills.

The solution was yet another change in venue. The mission moved to Second Avenue and N.W. Fifth Street.

By 1945, when World War II ended, thousands of soldiers returned home to an unemployment problem. Soon, the homelessness issue was again on the rise.

Meanwhile, the mission in 1949 was on the move again, this

time back to its former home near South Miami Avenue.

Schleucher was 71 at that time in 1949, and he still worked full-time — aside from the mission — in order to provide for his family. After work, he came to the mission, preaching on a nearly nightly basis.

Sadly, Schleucher died in 1952.

THE ASH FAMILY

Greatfully the baton was passed to the Ash family. Between the years of 1947-1970, Rev. McKinley Ash and his wife Marguerite H. Ash along with the help of his son George and daughter-in-law Connie took the reins of the ministry.

Prior to running the mission the Ash's came to Miami in 1925 and began a ministry to the jails and hospitals. They took up the challenge of rescue ministry and became leaders who would bring about the formal incorporation of the organization with its rented quarter on 150 West Flagler street.

The Ash's formed Miami Mission Association on December 11, 1947 and a charter was granted to the association in the chambers of Judge Marshal Wiseheart. The Miami Rescue Mission then became the DBA of the Association/Incorporation.

Under Ash's leadership the mission in 1954 was able to move from the rented headquarter on Flagler to a new purchased two-story building located at 140 NW First Street, where — initially — there were 140 beds.

In 1959, 66 more beds were added and plus a upgraded cafeteria and chapel area. Also in 1958 a building that could house a thrift store was purchased at 2233 NW 1st Court. This created a needed work rehabilitation program for the men and helped the in their recovery.

In 1969, still under the leadership of the Ash's a new residential and administrative building was built at 2250 NW 1st Avenue (which was behind the thrift store on NW 1st Court). This building was designed for the growing men's residential recovery program.

The same year, 1969, Zada Schleucher – who had remained active in mission work – passed away.

Rev. McKinley Ash retired in 1970 followed by interim directors and Allapatta Baptist Church holding the mission up.

That set the stage for Dr. Franklin Monroe Jacobs to become Executive Director of the mission in 1975 and, later, Reverend Ronald Brummitt in 2004.

HARD TIMES

The Miami Rescue Mission almost ceased to exist in the early 1970s, due primarily to financial difficulties.

"It was hanging by a thread," Jacobs said.

Jacobs, retired and living in Alabama at the time of this writing, recalls that the five-year period between the retirement of Ash and his taking over the mission was a time of turbulence and upheaval.

In fact, after the Miami Rescue Mission started facing overwhelming financial difficulties, the board of directors voted to place management of the mission over to the Allapattah Baptist Church. Jacobs, who was the music director of a large choir at that church, soon became part of the mission's board of directors.

Dr. Donald G. Manuel, the pastor of the Allapattah Baptist Church, was the chairman of the board of directors, and he was also the president of the Miami Rescue Mission.

Besides a lack of funds, the mission was dealing with eminent domain proceedings by Dade County, which was taking over several square blocks in downtown Miami for what was termed as "urban renewal". The mission's home at that time, at 140 West First Street, fell under that threat of eminent domain.

DETERMINED TO ENDURE

When Jacobs was, as he puts it, "the young man" on the mission's board of directors, he expressed the optimism that often comes with youth. He felt the mission could be saved, to which the rest of the board members said in unison: "Have at it."

Jacobs recruited his young friend, attorney Jeff A. Tew, and they set out to settle all legal claims and financial obligations that had been saddling the mission plus a major issue was the city had issued an "eminent domain" degree on the 140 West First Street.

Before the mission left their home at same address, Jacobs implored his friend, then-Dade County Mayor Stephen Clark, to let the mission stay at their spot downtown – rent free – for about seven months before that building was demolished.

This was crucial.

"We were flat busted," Jacobs said. "We didn't have anywhere to go. This gave us breathing room, a reprieve."

Given a clean slate financially, Jacobs started a fundraising campaign to be able to find a new home, and the rest is history.

Dr. Frank and Maxine Jacobs

With a love for the Lord and a passion for music, this Alabama native transformed the Miami Rescue Mission over a span of 33 years

Dr. Franklin Monroe Jacobs, who volunteered first and then ran the Miami Mission from 1975 until his retirement in 2006 has come full circle.

He was born in Ariton – located in southeastern Alabama – on June 25, 1936. And, after a lifetime of ministry in South Florida, Ariton is exactly where he and his wife live now that they are retired. In fact, Jacobs was born in his parents' home, and that's the same house where he now resides.

"Being born in your house was a common practice in the rural South at the time," Jacobs said. "To go to a hospital, you had to be very sick or badly injured."

Jacobs – who only had a high school diploma at the time – married his wife Maxine on Feb. 1, 1958. Jacobs was an insurance agent in Dothan, Alabama, and Maxine worked for the U.S. Army as a secretary/receptionist at their Fort Rucker dental clinic.

Jacobs had been out of high school four years when he decided he needed to make a change.

"I was not fulfilled working as an insurance agent," he said. "It was not my cup of tea.

"The minister of music at our church (Paul Tadlock) was a graduate of Howard College, and he had heard me sing. He told me, 'I believe God has His hand on you to do something special'."

Tadlock recommended Jacobs attend Howard College – now known as Samford University – located in Homewood, Alabama, which is a Birmingham suburb. The school, which pre-dates the Civil War, was founded in 1841.

Jacobs, after much prayerful consideration, made his decision to return to school.

"I felt very strongly that this was the direction I should go, to get educated and prepared," he said. "I let Maxine know, and she said that whatever I felt was the leading of the Lord, she was willing to accept.

"We both resigned our jobs and loaded all our earthly belongings onto a U-Haul trailer and my '57, sky-blue Chevrolet, and we were off to Birmingham with no place to live and no prospects for a job."

Perhaps it's appropriate at this juncture in Jacobs' story to remind us that the songwriter Jon Bon Jovi wrote a song called "Livin' On A Prayer" that describes perfectly what he and Maxine were experiencing at that time:

> *"We've got to hold on to what we've got. It doesn't make a difference if we make it or not. We've got each other, and that's a lot. For love, we'll give it a shot. ... Take my hand.*

We'll make it, I swear. Woah, we're living on a prayer."

Pretty soon, Jacobs and Maxine had reached Howard College.

With its rolling hills and stately Georgian Colonial architecture, the college was an oasis of serenity, beauty and higher learning. But, as gorgeous as it was, there was still that matter of where to live and how to pay for this new adventure.

So … just as they were driving around the Howard College area, Jacobs spotted a sign in the front yard of a house that read:

"Apartment for rent."

As it turns out, the widow who lived there had made the upstairs of her home into a stand-alone apartment, and it came equipped with a mesmerizingly panoramic view of the mountains. The apartment, which sat in the tree line, rented for $24 every two weeks, and Jacobs and Maxine took it immediately.

With their home secured, Jacobs contacted one of the local leaders of the Baptist church, introducing himself by phone. Jacobs told the man he was looking for part-time work as a music director at a church, and, as God was leading, there was an opening in near-by Tarrant.

Jacobs drove there, interviewed and was hired on the spot. The pay was $40 per week.

Meanwhile, Maxine got hired as a secretary for a trucking company, but it wasn't a good fit.

"She would come home crying every day," Jacobs said. "The atmosphere, the foul language – the whole thing that goes on in that industry."

Thankfully, just a few weeks later, Maxine got a notice that there was an opening with the U.S. Treasury Department in downtown Birmingham.

Maxine got the job and was so proficient that, pretty soon, they offered her a promotion. But because the new job would've required her to move to Washington D.C., she declined.

By 1962, Jacobs had earned his Bachelor's degree at Howard, majoring in voice.

From there, Jacobs went to the New Orleans Baptist Theological Seminary, earning a Master's degree in church music.

"New Orleans was a distant land for a country boy like me from Lower Alabama," Jacobs said. "But it was all in God's plans. Maxine was willing, once again, to pack up and go with me, this time to New Orleans. She got transferred to a job on Canal Street with the U.S. Department of Agriculture."

After graduating in 1964, Jacobs moved even further away from home, to South Florida. He was hired as the minister of music by the North Pompano Baptist Church.

"We decided to go to South Florida for a look-see," Jacobs said of the interview process. "The (North Pompano Baptist Church) gave us a unanimous vote and called us to come serve there."

MUSIC BRINGS PEOPLE TOGETHER

A classically trained vocalist and pianist, Jacobs organized and directed all the music at that church for two years.

In 1966, Jacobs moved to Miami and became the Minister

of Music at Allapattah Baptist Church, where he was ordained a dozen years later.

It was at the mission that Jacobs picked up his nickname: "Dr. J." That nickname has long been a source of amusement since a former NBA star, Hall of Famer Julius Erving, already had that moniker.

"My nickname came from my black friends in the (Miami Rescue Mission) program," Jacobs said. "It was an affectionate name they would yell across the parking lot when they would see me walking around campus.

"My staff picked it up, and it stuck. We would have some big laughs about it because of the contrast. The 'other Dr. J' is a famous, 6-foot-7 basketball player, and I'm a 5-9 white guy with a doctorate degree in church music."

While in Miami, Jacobs' prior training at the New Orleans Baptist Theological Seminary came into play. It was at the seminary where Jacobs was taught in real-world settings in addition to his classroom studies.

Students were expected to complete field missions so that they could put into practice what they were learning in theory.

During Jacobs' first semester, he was assigned to the psych ward of a hospital. His mission was to sit with the patients on the ninth floor. Jacobs would talk to them and also pray with them if they desired.

There was a chapel on the same floor, and Jacobs would invite patients there, and that's where he would lead them in old hymns as part of a short service, including a Bible sermon or message.

For the next semester, Jacobs was assigned to the local rescue mission, which was run by the New Orleans Baptist Association. Jacobs and other volunteers would give food and clothing to the homeless, helping them get off the street so that they could turn their lives around.

"Coming from the country, I didn't know what I was getting myself into," Jacobs said. "It was January when the semester started, and there were some pretty cold nights in New Orleans that winter.

"When I walked into the chapel for the first time, I saw about 75 men wrapped up in blankets and old coats. They were all bearded, and the heat was going pretty high.

"The aroma and odor from these men knocked you down when you walked in the room. But I met some of the most interesting people from just about every walk of life.

"They had been doctors and lawyers, laborers and misfits. But I just found them to be so appreciative of everything we did for them. They loved the singing at chapel service, and, to me, it brought back memories of my childhood, going to church and hearing these old hymns.

"This was my first introduction to homelessness and rescue work. I grew up in a dry county. People who wanted to drink had to go to another county. Where I lived, we didn't have a town drunk. We didn't even have a town, it was so small. We lived out in peanut fields with hogs and cows as well as cotton and corn.

"At first, seeing the homeless was quite a shock. But as I

look back, I see the hand of God in all of this."

Jacobs' connection with the homeless in Miami began one night after chapel service in Allapattah, where he was approached by B.L. Helm, who was one of the leading members of the church.

Helm, who was also on the board of directors of the Miami Rescue Mission, invited Jacobs to tend to the homeless. This was meant as sort of a test, not knowing that Jacobs had experience in this field from his days in New Orleans.

Jacobs passed that test and many more over the decades. He proved his value by caring for everyone he encountered. But, over the years, things changed. Originally, the profile of a homeless person was mainly white men who were alcoholics.

But, as the years passed by, the median age of the homeless got lower. More people of color started entering the program, and that was especially true once the crack epidemic hit. More women – many of them escaping physical and sexual abuse – and their children came to the mission.

It would've been easy for Jacobs to have been repulsed by some of the things he saw. But he viewed the homeless as simply people who had lost their way and could be redeemed with a little help and God's love.

"They were homeless, but, often, they were highly educated and culturally alert people," Jacobs said. "The common denominator was that alcohol had taken a toll and destroyed their lives.

"Over the years, we saw people you wouldn't expect – former professional athletes, superstars. It would just break your heart."

LOOKING FOR A NEW HOME

By 1976, word had gotten out that the Miami Rescue Mission was looking for a new home, and a big, burly man approached Jacobs with a simple question:

"Why don't you buy my hotel?"

This was the Royal Hotel, which was in no way fit for a king or a queen. Located downtown at 716 North Miami Avenue, the Royal Hotel was a flop house, used primarily by street hookers who aggressively flagged down customers in front of the property.

Jacobs negotiated a purchase price of the Royal Hotel for $95,000, including a $20,000 down payment.

But there was just one problem: Jacobs didn't have the 20 grand.

"We were operating on faith," Jacobs said. "I had left a secure field (as a church music director). I had turned down opportunities from churches from all over the country."

Within two months, that faith was restored.

Jacobs had returned to his office one day when his wife notified him that a trust officer from a bank on Miami Beach had called. Jacobs – who remembers his name as only "Mr. Simmons" -- returned the call.

As it turns out, the Miami Rescue Mission had received an anonymous donation. A gentleman, who had been a supporter of the cause, left the money in his will as a living legacy.

"Mr. Simmons told me that all I had to do was sign a few papers, and I would receive a cashier's check in a few days," Jacobs said. "I swallowed hard and asked him for the amount of the donation."

As it turns out, God knew exactly what was needed to purchase the Royal Hotel, almost to the last penny, because the donation was for $20,900. By the time Jacobs gave the $20,000 down payment and also shelled out what was needed for stamps and other fees, all he had left was 25 cents for the parking meter.

Once the sale was complete, the next step was to clean up and refurbish the Royal Hotel – and that was no small task.

This was a three-story hotel with no elevators. Jacobs and some volunteers rented a huge dumpster – the kind used on construction sites – and started ripping up the carpet. Next, they started tossing out all the mattresses that were riddled with fleas, germs, roaches, rat droppings and every other nasty thing imaginable. Everything went into that dumpster, and much of it was just tossed out the windows.

Next, professionals were brought in to fix the bathrooms and refurbish the building that would become home for the Miami Rescue Mission from 1976 to 1985.

ANOTHER MOVE

By 1985, however, the mission had to move again because of eminent domain, this time to make way for what was to be the new home of the NBA Basketbal Arena (Miami Heat). Construction of Miami Arena began on August 4, 1986 until it, too, was torn down in 2008.

With what was once the Royal Hotel reduced to rubble, the Miami Rescue Mission once again searched for a new home, operating out of rental properties for a couple of years.

Finally, in 1989, the Mission had found a permanent home

at 2020 NW 1st Avenue, but how that place came to be is a story onto itself.

At that time, the block featured a manufacturing building at 2010 NW 1st Avenue and a business that made and sold tile at 2060 NW 1st Avenue.

In the middle, there was vacant land, where Jacobs decided he would design and construct one of the first buildings in the country built specifically for the homeless.

When the project was near completion, Jacobs contacted City of Miami administrators to find out what his new address would be … only to find out that he would be able to choose any even number between 2010 and 2060.

It's not often a person gets to choose his own address, so, in an unusual situation such as this, Jacobs did what came naturally.

He turned to the Bible: John 20:20, a passage in which Jesus speaks to His disciples after His hands had been nailed to the cross and after His resurrection.

"He showed them his hands and side. The disciples were overjoyed when they saw the Lord."

Jacobs found a correlation to that Bible passage – 20-20 vision is perfect and so it is perfection at 2020 NW 1st Avenue when those who had been homeless finally see Christ.

"We introduce them to the Lord," Jacobs said. "And when they see that the Lord loves them and has a plan for their lives, it is perfect spiritual vision.

"Before they came to us, they were sad, despondent and without hope. But then they see the Lord, and they are made glad."

PART 2

FINDING SALVATION

—

Graduates Of The Miami Rescue Mission

In the following miracle stories, meet people who beat the odds with the help of God's grace and the Miami Rescue Mission

Alex Chaviano

He defied death – as a drug dealer, a cocaine addict and as someone on the run from the mafia – before getting saved by the mission.

Running from a Colombian drug cartel, battling an addiction to crack cocaine and spending one month near death and in a coma – Alex Chaviano has known the depths of despair.

What has happened to him since, however, likely qualifies as a miracle.

The Miami Rescue Mission saved Chaviano's life. He graduated from the mission in 2007, and Chaviano, 61, now serves as an ordained minister and a case-manager supervisor at the men's center in Miami.

Chaviano, whose father was murdered in Mexico in 1996, has found his calling at the Miami Rescue Mission. With help from the mission, he earned a Bachelor's degree in Theology from the Assemblies of God. He is a certified addiction counselor, and he also earned a doctorate degree in Divinity from the Latin University of Theology.

"This was divine intervention," Chaviano said of his life. "When I got ordained on June 19, 2014, it was beyond coincidence. I lost my biological father exactly nine years earlier, but then I gained my spiritual father in God almighty.

"This mission is all about saving and restoring people's lives, and Christianity is salvation."

Clearly, Chaviano has found peace and is giving back to his community. But to understand the serenity Chaviano has found, it is necessary to comprehend the chaos that he somehow survived for the first several chapters of his life.

Born in Santa Clara in the virtual center of Cuba, Chaviano was six years old when he came to live in Miami. After some moving around, he settled in White Plains, New York, where he married his first wife.

All was well until Chaviano started using – and then dealing – cocaine. This was during the 1980s, when the TV show Miami Vice was omnipresent, a prime example of art imitating what was just then exploding in American life.

"I was head deep into trafficking cocaine, using my business as a front to cover all the money coming in," Chaviano said. "I never got arrested for trafficking, but I did five years in prison on a murder charge.

"Ultimately, I was exonerated. I won the case after all that time in jail awaiting trial. I could've gotten 25 years had I pled guilty and life in prison had I lost. That was God's first intervention in my life."

Liberated from jail, Chaviano wasn't free of trouble.

When he was finally released from prison, Chaviano went on the run from a Colombian cartel that was bent on revenge for a drug deal gone bad.

"I was in fear for my life, and I had to divorce my wife to

try to keep her safe," Chaviano said. "I then came back to Miami, and I went underground for a year."

Staying with a relative, Chaviano didn't make so much as a phone call for that year.

With all his money gone, Chaviano finally started to resurface, working as a parking valet. But then he started using drugs again, and that led to a horrific car crash in December of 2000, leaving Chaviano with 19 fractures in his jaw.

"Doctors had to sew my tongue back together," Chaviano said. "I was in a coma for a month, and they were about to pull the plug. My health insurance was running out, and I think my life flashed in front of me."

Even so, Chaviano didn't seem to learn much of a lesson -- at least not at that time – because he started smoking crack cocaine two months after getting out of the hospital.

At that point, Chaviano's addiction controlled his life, and he was arrested four times in just one month, all for drug possession. After that fourth arrest, he was sentenced to one year in jail.

But even before discovering crack cocaine, Chaviano's life had already spun out of control. He had lost his father on June 19, 1996. His father, who worked in the import/export business, had been strangled and was found naked and tied to a chair.

Two years later, Chaviano tried to commit suicide, drinking all his mother's medication. However, his brother returned home sooner than expected and found Chaviano on the floor, saving his life.

But after he got sentenced to jail following his fourth arrest on charges of possession of crack cocaine, that was the proverbial last straw for his family. He was no longer welcome at his mother's house.

"I was a parasite leaching off of her," Chaviano said. "My brother told me, 'You don't exist to us anymore'."

Chaviano, with no other options, started living in his car, a 1996 Jeep. Pretty soon, he lost that, too, and the street became his permanent address.

The turning point for Chaviano came on June 19, 2005, the nine-year anniversary of his father's death. That's when he finally went to the Miami Rescue Mission for help, fortuitously grabbing the last available bed on that day.

"I have so much evidence of God working in my life," Chaviano said. "Exactly nine years later, I was ordained as a minister."

Prior to finding the mission, Chaviano had searched for God in the traditional place – church – but his addiction always got in the way.

"I remember one time there was this husband and wife that wanted to help, but this addiction is a monster," Chaviano said. "They didn't know how to deal with this animal.

"After church service, they gave me $20 spending money, and I used it to get high. Then I thought, 'What is this? Why do I still want to smoke crack? God doesn't care about me.'

"I had a lot of resentment."

Once he found the mission, however, he discovered that

God hadn't abandoned him. In fact, he learned that God had a purpose for him – to help others.

Chaviano lived at the mission for eight years, but it wasn't easy. Antonio Villasuso was his counselor in those early years at the mission, and it was like taming a wild bronco.

"I was a hard case," Chaviano said. "I was written up 14 times for stealing, lying and other rules violations.

"Antonio was very tough on me. He kicked me out of the mission once for about 24 hours."

Chaviano spent that one rainy night right outside the mission, sleeping on pavement. He remembers a prostitute coming by and offering him crack cocaine, but he was able to resist the temptation.

"The devil is a liar, bro," Chaviano said. "That was a scary night. But I was determined to change my life."

Drug free, Chaviano visited Villasuso the next day.

"I got on my knees and begged him to take me back," Chaviano said. "Anthony grabbed me by my neck, and that's how he broke me.

"Getting free of addiction is a process."

These days, it's Chaviano who is the disciplinarian. These days, it's Chaviano who is saving those who are lost.

Happily, Chaviano reconciled with his mother and brother, a joyful reunion that happened about two years after he came to the Miami Rescue Mission.

"As you move up in the (addiction recovery) program, you get certain privileges," Chaviano said.

"On my 67th day in the program, I was given some brief hours off. My brother allowed me to visit my mom. I took two buses and a train and then walked half a mile to see her for 15 minutes.

"I cried and told her I was sorry. I hugged her, and then I had to go back, but it was worth the sacrifice getting there."

Chaviano said his difficult experiences have helped him minister the men he now supervises.

"Addiction is a bio-chemical brain disease," Chaviano said. "I went to college because i wanted to know more about the psychological aspect of my addiction.

"I wanted to learn how to deal with myself but also how to help other people in the same situation. It wasn't about getting a fancy degree or title. I wanted to know God and know about my addiction."

In 2019, Chaviano was diagnosed with lung cancer. He endured six months of chemotherapy and lost half a lung, but the disease is in remission.

Chaviano said he still deals with physical pain from his fight against cancer, but it's nothing he can't handle.

"If there is not a purpose in your life, then life has no meaning," he said. "This is the road I've had to travel to find my purpose, which is to help others."

Gary Cooper

———

From the high life to losing a son and falling to the depths of despair, he found salvation at the mission

Gary Cooper shares a name with a famed actor who won two Academy Awards in the 1930s and 1940s.

But the Gary Cooper in our story has had no such glamour.

Instead, Cooper was born in 1973 in the southern half of Miami Dade County. He grew up with a father who was in and out of his life, "drugging and drinking," according to his son.

Cooper's mother worked hard at various jobs in an effort to provide for her son. She is now retired, but, as hard as she worked, she never could keep her son in line.

The Cooper family lived in the projects back then, in a town called Goulds, near Homestead. Cooper dropped out of Miami Southridge High School in the ninth grade and began hanging out in street corners, smoking and selling weed.

This career choice wasn't popular with his mother, who gave him an ultimatum: Live by her rules … or leave.

Cooper chose the latter and went to live with another weed dealer. This was in 1989. By 1990, Cooper had moved up to selling cocaine, and he had already been arrested, spending a few days in jail.

In 1992, Hurricane Andrew hit, and Cooper moved from Goulds to Miami's hard-core Liberty City.

"It was from country life to the inner city," Cooper said.

Life in Liberty City was lived at a faster pace, and the drugs were harder, too. Cooper started selling heroin and making serious money.

In 1992, at age 19, Cooper said he was selling $80,000 worth of drugs in an average week, netting him a profit of about $4,000.

Cooper had three cars at that time – a 1979 Chevy, a 1979 Cadillac Fleetwood and a 1967 Camaro. It was not unusual for him to deck out one of his cars with an $8,000 stereo system or fancy rims.

"I had cars, women, jewelry," Cooper said. "The lifestyle was partying and strip clubs."

But the fast times wouldn't last long.

Cooper had a son in 1995, but the boy died of kidney failure four years later.

"I was affected," Cooper said. "I wasn't with his mom, but I would go by and spend time with him."

Feelings of guilt and grief overcame Cooper. Already involved in using and selling drugs, Cooper self-medicated by using cocaine.

"One night, I was out of cocaine, so I started using crack," Cooper said. "I figured it was more or less the same, but it was a lot worse.

"Everything spiraled out of control. I'm trying to hustle

(selling drugs), but I was using my own product, smoking out of a crack pipe.

"That was rock bottom – no money, eating out of dumpsters, stealing.

"I would sleep in abandoned apartment buildings or those under construction. On Friday nights, when construction crews were closed for the weekend, I would sleep in those buildings until Monday morning.

"During the week, I would be in the projects, working for different drug guys, basically being a slave. I was too busy to sleep. I was broke and high all the time. And when you're high, you don't need to sleep. You are just chasing the next high."

By Christmas Day in 2000, Cooper had begun to question his life choices. He was crashing at an abandoned apartment when he saw and heard the happy squealing of children riding their new bikes.

"I broke down crying," Cooper said. "I thought, 'What the hell am I doing? When did I envision this was my life?'

"I sold crack cocaine. I knew what that drug did to people, and I still sold crack. I was thinking, 'What is wrong with me?'"

Cooper wanted to change, but he didn't know how.

He knew there was a bench warrant out for his arrest, so he went to a pay phone, dialed 911 and tried to turn himself in so he could clean himself up while in jail.

But when the police officers arrived, they checked their computers and did not find a warrant out for Cooper.

That's when Cooper went to Plan B. He walked to an

Amoco gas station. He stuffed his fingers into his shirt and claimed to have a gun. He asked the attendant at the gas station's convenience store for money, purposely trying to get himself arrested.

The plan worked – sort of.

A police officer happened to walk in and arrested Cooper, handcuffing him and calling for backup. When those officers arrived, one of them took a look at Cooper – dirty and pretty obviously homeless – and said:

"It's Christmas. Let him go."

Cooper told the officers he needed help, and one of them finally took action.

He drove Cooper to the busway. He told the bus driver to take Cooper to the Dadeland South train station, which would take him to Crisis Center.

The cop waited until Cooper got on the bus and the doors closed. Once at Dadeland South, the bus driver walked Cooper to the train station.

Cooper made it to Crisis Center, where he was handed a clipboard to fill out information.

It was hardly the personal touch Cooper needed, and, when he spotted another homeless man walk in, he handed that guy his clipboard and left for Jackson Hospital.

At Jackson, Cooper was directed to the Miami Rescue Mission, and that changed everything.

"It was 20-something years ago, but I still remember I got there at 4:30 p.m. because that was the time that they were serving food," Cooper said. "I will never forget the first person I met there was Ed Oakles, who was a guest services staff member.

"I told Ed I needed help. He said: 'OK, let's get you a shower and something to eat'."

The shower Cooper took that night was nothing routine. In those days, when Cooper was getting high and living on the street, it was nothing unusual for him to go four months without a bath of any kind.

"I smelled awful," Cooper said. "It took one month for my skin to go back to its original color. It wasn't brown like now. It was burnt black from caked on dirt.

"That first shower felt so good."

Cooper, who is 5-foot-10, now weighs 235 pounds. But, back then, at the height of his constant drug-taking, no-eating, no-sleeping lifestyle, Cooper weighed an unhealthy 119 pounds.

It took him two days at the mission before he got his appetite back. Cooper stayed with the Miami Rescue Mission program and graduated in October of 2001. He then started working for the mission, building scaffolds for construction crews.

With the money he earned, Cooper bought a 1993 Mercedes Benz that had just been donated to the mission.

Cooper left the mission in 2005, renting an efficiency in Richmond Heights.

However, as with many recovering addicts, staying on the right path is often something less than a straight road.

In 2007, Cooper ran into an old friend who told him all the money he was making by selling drugs in Key West. Cooper took the bait, but he was soon arrested for selling crack cocaine, spending seven months in jail.

Cooper was released from prison in October of 2008, and he was quickly met with a stark reality. His car had been repossessed. He had been evicted from his apartment.

Everything he had worked so hard to earn was gone.

Naturally, Cooper went back to the mission.

"To me," Cooper said, "the Miami Rescue Mission is like grandma's house – it's family."

It really is family for Cooper, who was doing volunteer work at the mission's Broward Outreach Center where he met Vanessa, who is now his wife. They met around Christmas 2009 and married on May 14, 2010.

Vanessa had been working as an Outreach Center volunteer for nearly three years when she met Cooper. He had been struggling to find a job. She encouraged him, and, when he found work, she was thrilled.

"I guess he started giving me little hints (about wanting to date her), but I didn't know," Vanessa said. "I kept praying.

"One day, he wrote me this beautiful letter. I prayed over the letter and told God to lead me. I told God: 'I don't know how you want me to be in his life.'

"To make a long story short, we started going to church together. He was very humble. I knew there was something special about him."

Vanessa, who has three grown children, knew a little bit about addiction before meeting Cooper. She had a cousin in New York who had struggled with substances.

As for her own path to God, it started when one of her two sons was 11 years old.

"I was a single mom, struggling," she said. "I wasn't a Christian just yet. My son was watching a church service. He was struggling in school.

"I said to myself, 'I have to visit this church.' I eventually went to that church and got saved. I became a Christian, and they had a program to volunteer. I started feeding the homeless in Plantation. I found this compassion I never knew I had, but I figured I needed to do more.

"All my corporate jobs with Tiffany's and Black+Decker suddenly meant nothing. Then it came to me in a dream to apply to work at the Miami Rescue Mission, even at half my former salary.

"I had never done a job like this before, but I said, 'OK, God, I'm going to let you lead me.'

"It has been the most rewarding job I've ever had. I don't think you can ever have a bad day when you hear these stories from the people at the mission. I'm so blessed. My problems don't compare.

"There are really good people here who just need to be encouraged and loved on."

Cooper, of course, was one of those people who needed love and encouragement. In 2010, Cooper started working at AutoNation Nissan, detailing cars.

By 2012, he had moved up to the sales department, and he and his wife were living at one of the mission's houses off of Sheridan Street in Hollywood.

In 2015, Cooper made a decision that was close to his heart. Even though he was making more money at AutoNation Nissan, he went back to his "family" – the mission. He took a job as one of the guest-services supervisors at the Broward Outreach Center.

"It gave me the opportunity to work on my recovery and the recovery of others," Cooper said. "It was a no-brainer."

Cooper now owns a house in Liberty City, and he and his wife are committed to the mission's cause.

"I'm not leaving the Miami Rescue Mission," Cooper said. "My step-daughter, who is 19, also works for the mission as a donor-services assistant."

Cooper's past experiences are a useful part of his job now, and he uses the painful lessons he has learned to try to help the recovering addicts he encounters on a daily basis.

"The people I deal with now at the mission – they all know my story," Cooper said. "My story is inspiring to them. They want to emulate what I have accomplished."

Cooper is grateful to the Miami Rescue Mission.

"I wouldn't have my family or anything I have now if not for the mission," Cooper said. "They saved my life."

Anthony Durden

———

Straight out of Compton – and into gang life – he finally got clean and sober with the help of the Miami Rescue Mission

Anthony Eugene Durden has been cut and slashed by a fellow prison inmate's razor blade, seen his own blood gushing out of the side of his face.

He's been chased by gang members, police dogs and helicopters, spending 15 years in and out jail.

And he's gone from drug dealer to crack addict, falling so low that he resorted to eating out of garbage cans.

But, through it all, God never gave up on him. And, in turn, Durden – who grew up playing the drums in church choirs – said he heard God's call, even in his lowest moments.

"Back in 2002, I was homeless in Miami, strung out on crack," Durden said. "I was trying to get high, but I kept hearing God's voice.

"He was telling me, 'Come out.'

"I believe I had an epiphany."

That epiphany eventually led Durden to the Miami Rescue Mission, which helped him turn his life around.

Durden, now 50, has been clean and sober for 16 years. He's

happily married, he has a steady job, and he's also a motivational speaker, ministering to everyone from death-row inmates to at-risk youth.

But before we reveal more about Durden's current life, it's worth taking a look at how he got here.

The son of Brilla and Bobby Durden, he was born in Miami. But when Brilla and Bobby got divorced, Durden – who was six years old at the time – went to live with his mom in Compton, California.

At first, Durden made a fairly smooth transition. He was a talented athlete – football, basketball, track and baseball – and popular.

But Durden had his first experience using drugs and alcohol at age 13, and that started an addiction that lasted 21 years.

"I took my first hit of marijuana when I was in the sixth grade," Durden said. "I found my stepfather's stash. From that point on, I smoked weed every day before I went to school."

The gang life was thus a natural connection for Durden. As it turned out, many of the kids in his neighborhood were part of the notorious Crips gang, and Durden found what he thought was a home there.

A good student, Durden dropped out of high school in the 10th grade, committing himself fully to the gang life.

"I was making thousands of dollars a day selling drugs," Durden said. "Ultimately, that's why I quit school."

Later, Durden got a job working security at Los Angeles International Airport. After work, he would sell drugs. At times, he would sell drugs at the airport, too.

When he turned 18, his mother sent him to Miami to live with his father, Bobby, in hopes that a change of scenery could get him back on the right path.

"The move helped me reconnect with my father," Durden said. "But my lifestyle in Miami wasn't much different than in Compton."

Drug-dealing and drug-using go hand in hand, Durden said, and, by age 30, he was hooked on crack cocaine. Once that happened, all his money went away, and it was only a matter of time before he became homeless.

Soon, the arrests started piling up, too, – drug possession, burglary, armed robbery, grand theft and battery on a law-enforcement officer, among other charges.

"I was living a lifestyle of criminality," Durden said. "I was in countless shootouts, high-speed chases and car crashes. I had guns pulled on me … I could have easily lost my life."

But God had a different plan for Durden.

"Toward the end of my drug addiction, when I would get high, I would start preaching about God," Durden said. "I think I preached my first sermon at a crack house."

There wasn't much of an audience, however. When Durden started preaching, the other addicts fled.

"I would turn around," Durden said, "and I would find myself alone. Nobody wanted to get high with a preacher."

At that point, Durden would usually start walking aimlessly through the streets of downtown Miami.

"I'd walk for many miles," Durden said. "One day, I stumbled onto the steps of the Miami Rescue Mission, although I didn't know that's what it was at the time.

"I just knew that I saw this guy. He and I used to run the streets, selling drugs and getting high together. But now he was dressed in a suit and tie, and he had this glow about him.

"He asked me if I wanted to come into the program. I had no idea what he was saying."

Even so, Durden -- tired, hungry and strung out -- accepted the offer. But he hadn't yet grasped the concept of turning his life over to God.

Instead, Durden entered the mission for three days, sleeping for most of his stay.

After that, he left.

"But at least I knew there was somewhere I could go," Durden said.

Durden soon found his way back to the mission, and he was about to graduate from the Alpha program.

In fact, he had been clean and sober for months, but the call of addiction is strong, and Durden relapsed. He left the program and got himself arrested again, this time for burglary and drug possession.

"I did 10 more months in jail, and that was the worst time in my life," Durden said. "I was angry at myself. I realized I had changed, and my old life was no longer attractive to me.

"I figured out that I had to learn how to handle freedom. After all, in prison I conformed to their rules. Why couldn't I conform to the rules at the mission?

"So, I worked on being accountable and responsible. That was the epiphany that has kept me on the path of sobriety for the past 16 years."

Durden graduated from the mission's Regeneration Program in 2006.

The next year, he became the president of the Christian Men's Club Corporation and of SHEAR Inc, which stands for Sharing Hope Empowerment and Reaction.

For the past 14 years, he has worked as a lighting technician, a job he got with the help of a friend he met at the mission.

"Before I got that job, I didn't know how to plug lights or how they operated," said Durden, who works for Chauvet Lighting. "I got in on a favor. God gave me the hook-up."

Durden also works hard to give back to those less fortunate. He is a spiritual advisor at The Circle of Brotherhood. He is a member of Koinonia Workshop Center & Village, under the leadership of Pastor Eric H. Jones Jr.

In addition, Durden has helped organize countless community-service events, feeding the homeless, participating in a "Stop the Violence" prayer walk, and hosting Bible studies at the place that saved his life, the Miami Rescue Mission.

Durden has a passion for helping young people. He serves as a spiritual advisor for the Miramar High School football team and performs the same role for the Miami Gardens Optimist program.

"Most of my work is done in the trenches," Durden said. "I minister in the streets.

"I tell my story, and I give them hope and inspiration. I can paint a picture of where their lives are now and where they are going if they don't change."

In fact, Durden's community service played a large role in the courtship of his wife, Deshawn, whom he married on April 4, 2018.

"I first saw her on Facebook, singing praises to the Lord," Durden said. "Most of our dating time was spent doing community service, feeding the homeless, for example.

"She became my partner and my helpmate even before she became my wife."

Ron and Marilyn Brummitt have also played a big role in Durden's life.

"(Marilyn) was the first person who showed me how to share my testimony," said Durden, whose next plan is to get his high school GED and then start college. "I was working as a receptionist at the mission at the time. When she had guests, she would say, 'Anthony, can you share your testimony?'

"At that time, I didn't even know what testimony was. But I soon learned that my testimony could help others, and it also allowed me to break the barriers of the negative stigma of drug addiction.

"When I realized my testimony empowered others, it helped me break free. It was healing for me."

Ron Brummitt was also a big influence for Durden. However, at first, the idea of a faith-based mission was intimidating for Durden.

"I grew up in church, but people didn't talk about drug addiction back then," Durden said. "So, when I got to the mission, I was thinking, 'How are they going to help someone as sick as me?'

"But the staff at the mission was so real and raw. Knowing that Ron Brummitt had been down the same perilous road of addiction as I had been ... that was inspirational.

"Before that, I had never thought someone who had been as nasty and as low as I had been, and, then, look at them now, as counselors.

"I believe that common bond is what has built the fellowship of the Miami Rescue Mission."

Bo Rico Hall

Virtually abandoned by his single mother, he ran wild, ending up with a drug addiction and suicidal feelings ... before finally finding peace

Borinquen "Bo Rico" Hall never knew his father and still doesn't know a single detail about him.

Hall's mother, as painful as it is for him to admit, abandoned him for much of his childhood, allowing him to run the streets of South Beach – unsupervised – starting at the age of eight.

Born in San Juan, Puerto Rico in 1974, Hall moved to South Beach with his mother when he was three months old. She was 30, and she wasn't up to the task of caring for her son.

Hungry, poor and often left with various babysitters, Hall soon ventured out to the beach, alone, breakdancing for tips and hustling for money any way he could.

By the age of 11, Hall began smoking cigarettes and drinking beer. Soon after that, he was getting high on weed every day.

"I vividly remember my friends who had parents while I was pretty much lonely," Hall said. "I didn't have a father. My mom was in and out."

Elementary school was a safe haven for Hall. It was a place where he could get a meal and associate with other children.

School, at that time, was a place where he could feel normal.

But, pretty soon, being unsupervised took its toll on Hall. By age 14, Hall had a mouth full of gold teeth.

"Who does that?" said Hall, incredulous at his own misguided youth. "I hustled so much money back then. But I was a minor, and this dentist – even though I had no parental supervision – put in these gold teeth as long as I had the money."

By the start of his 11th-grade year, Hall dropped out of Miami Beach High School.

"I was homeless by my early teens," Hall said. "My mom disowned me. She didn't care back then. I remember crying to her for help.

"Because of that, I wasn't focused on school. I ended up being sent to juvenile detention."

By his early 20s, Hall was strung out on cocaine and was arrested for "a couple of misdemeanors", mostly having to do with his homelessness.

At that time, Hall could see no way out of his misery.

"I was suicidal," he said. "I came close to dying a couple of times. I tried to kill myself by doing a lot of cocaine. I overdosed a couple of times and got sent to Jackson Hospital, where they revived me.

"But I just went right back to the streets. ... I got shot a few times, but I just didn't care.

"I would go on bad acid trips. I would be tripping for eight to 10 hours. Being on acid made me paranoid. I would find myself on the roof of a tall building, thinking everybody was out to get me."

Thankfully, Hall didn't jump.

During that time, Hall – who had no upbringing in religion – remembers praying to God to help rid him of his destructive thoughts and habits.

At this time, Hall was homeless, sleeping often at Miami Beach's Flamingo Park. And, perhaps because of his search for God – but also because he was physically hungry -- Hall found himself at a Miami Beach church, Calvary Christian.

The good people at the Calvary Christian chapel often put out a spread of doughnuts and coffee for their parishioners and those in the community, and Hall availed himself to that sustenance, speaking to no one.

Hall came to fill his belly, but – as it turned out – God filled his heart, too.

God performed a miracle on Hall, and it all came about because of a married couple from London -- Georgia and Frank Gittings-Hart.

"They befriended me," said Hall, who was 26 years old at the time. "They tried to lift me up and encourage me."

Hall heard them, but it took two years for the message to truly sink in and hit its mark.

"Within that time, I was on the street, and I would sometimes call Georgia and Frank," Hall said. "I would tell them, 'I haven't slept or eaten in days.'

"They would come and get me. They would feed me and allow me to take a shower and sleep. They showed me compassion, love and empathy."

Hall said he had never felt that love before. His mother, he said, was "cold-hearted" back then.

Georgia and Frank Gittings-Hart were different, however.

"They told me they saw me as their son," Hall said. "They saw me as a lost boy who had a lot of love in his heart but just needed some help.

"As time went on, I started listening to them and trusting them."

The turning point for Hall was the overdose death of one of his close childhood friends, Greg.

Hall had lost friends before – to everything from guns to addiction. It had happened so often that Hall had grown numb to the pain of those lost souls.

But when Greg died, Hall lost it mentally, spiraling out of control in a week-long haze of drugs and destruction.

After seven days of hell, Hall found his way to the North Beach home of Georgia and Frank.

"When they opened the door, I was done," Hall said. "I was ready for a change."

With the encouragement of Georgia and Frank, Hall – on Memorial Day weekend 2001 – checked into the Miami Rescue Mission.

Hall had his misgivings about the mission at first, however.

For starters, the mission was located in a neighborhood that was much rougher back then than it is now.

"I was thinking, 'Am I supposed to turn my life around here?'" Hall said. "Right outside the mission, there were crackheads, people getting jumped, beat down and killed."

Inside the mission, Hall found what he considered hardened ex-convicts who were pretty intimidating but were going through the program just like him.

Most importantly, Hall found numerous people who were committed to seeing him succeed. Among those people, Hall said, were Ron and Marilyn Brummitt.

"They showed me love and compassion," Hall said. "They gave me support. They said, 'You are not going out those doors. You are going to stay here until the miracle happens'."

Thanks to that support, Hall never relapsed. The miracle indeed happened.

The living arrangement at the mission was rough – Hall and the others who were going through the program slept in bunk beds with many men in the same room.

Still, Hall was able to persevere, staying at the mission for three years while he broke his drug habit, earned his GED and then an Associate's degree from Miami Dade College's Medical Campus.

In short, he got the training necessary to become an Emergency Medical Technician.

"Some people, when they find out I was living in a shelter for three years, feel sorry for me," Hall said. "A lot of people say, 'You were sleeping in a bunk bed in a room with a lot of dudes.'

"But the truth is that it was the best and most peaceful three years of my life.

"I was clean. I was fed. I had clean clothing. When I had medical appointments, they would pick me up and get me there.

"Because of all the cocaine I had consumed, I had a deviated septum in my nose. I needed a five-hour surgery, and I had a cast on my face that made me look like the 'Elephant Man'.

"But now I have a whole new nose. I had my gold teeth taken out. A whole new me was created."

Hall's earlier lifestyle had taken such a toll on him that he knew he couldn't stay at the mission for one week, one month or even one year without assistance. He needed help physically, mentally, emotionally ... and spiritually.

"The people at the mission never shoved a Bible down my throat," Hall said. "I found out that the most important thing is not religion. It's about a relationship with God."

That relationship has helped him through tough times, including the passing of a brother and a sister, neither of which he ever got to meet. His brother, Hall said, died of AIDS while living on the street in his native Trinidad and Tobago.

These days, Hall is a loving uncle to three nieces and two nephews – his sister's children – and he has worked to restore his relationship with his mother, who came to his graduation from the Miami Rescue Mission.

His nieces and nephews, by the way, live in Trinidad, and Hall has only seen them on Facetime chats.

"One of the greatest gifts I received at the mission was my relationship with God, and as long as I have Jesus Christ in my life, I can forgive," Hall said when asked about his mother.

"We all make mistakes in life. Before I got to the mission, I had a lot of hurt, anger and pain. But the mission helped create a new me."

Hall's mother is now 76 years old, and her health is not the best.

"The mission taught me to not look at her in a negative way," Hall said. "It wasn't her fault. I don't try to ask her questions about the past anymore. We are together now, and I just try to enjoy the moments.

"I'm not going to try to force information out of her. Now, it's more important that I take care of her, make sure she has food and medical attention."

Since 2004, Hall has been assisting the Miami Beach Police Department as a homeless outreach worker. He is the only civilian in the unit, working with four police officers.

Hall wakes up at 3:30 a.m., Monday through Friday, and he is quickly on the streets, reaching out to the homeless.

"At that hour," Hall said, "they are more open to accepting help."

As he encounters homeless people, Hall tries to get them to a shelter. He tries to get them health and behavioral treatment. He tries to help rescue girls who have been kidnapped and sold into the sex trade.

Anything to help people in need.

"When I meet someone who is homeless, sometimes they ask me, 'Do you know what it feels like to be hungry? Do you know what it feels like to live on the street?'" Hall said. "I tell them, 'Yes, I do.'"

Hall, who got married in 2013 and has a son from a previous relationship as well as two step-daughters, knows first-hand that his prior life experience has had an impact on the people he serves. When he was in the program as a recovering addict, he remembers being shocked to find out that Ron Brummitt had once been hooked on crack cocaine, living on the street.

"That carried a lot of weight," Hall said, "to have someone to relate to you.

"To know that Ron was once chronically homeless and hooked on drugs, that served as motivation because of where he's at now.

"I call Ron my father. His story has been a major part of why so many of us have turned our lives around.

"Ron never gave up on us. Ron is the reason why thousands of men, women and children who were formally homeless are now productive citizens in the community."

Grace Mission Bus

In late 20's **Grace Mission** merged with the Gospel Mission (group of church women) and become **Miami City Mission**, located at 538 N Miami Avenue.
Miami population: 110,637. During depresion years MCM cared for over 1,200 daily.

Rev. John and Zada Schleucher
Founders

(Graduate of Moody Bible Institute Interned at Pacific Garden Mission)

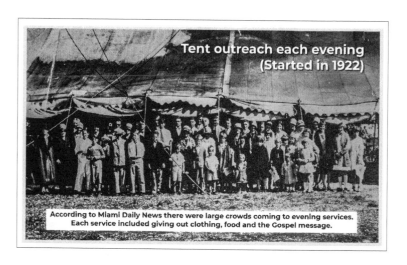

Tent outreach each evening
(Started in 1922)

According to Miami Daily News there were large crowds coming to evening services.
Each service included giving out clothing, food and the Gospel message.

First purchase of the Mission in 1955
Under the leadership of the Ashes

MIAMI   RESCUE   MISSION

140 NW First Street - First floor chapel and cafeteria and dormitory on second floor

Cafeteria of the Mission in the late 1950's

1947 - 1970 Leadership
Rev. McKinley Ash, Executive Director;
Marguerite Ash(wife), Welfare Director; and George D. Ash
(son), Treasurer; Constance Ash, Secretary

Located at The Little Flagler Street Mission (150 West Flagler)

1947 - 1970 Leadership
Rev. McKinley Ash, Executive Director;

February 1958   Vol. 1, No. 4

Board of Directors
Miami Mission Association, Inc.

Rev. McKinley Ash, Executive Director,
   Miami Rescue Mission

Marguerite Ash, Welfare Director.

George D. Ash, Assistant Director.

Otto Nelson .... President

Wm. H. Lee .... Vice President

George D. Ash .... Treasurer

Constance Ash .... Secretary

    Dr. W. J. Barge
    George Bradbury
    Rev. W. Maurice Fain
    B. Lafayette Helm
    Carl Sear
    Dr. Clyde L. Myers
    Rev. Orville Nelson
    Burton P. Nuckols
    William E. Stocking

MISSION SERVICES
7:30 p.m.   Daily
11:00 a.m.   Sunday

COUNTY JAIL SERVICES
10:00 a.m. - Wednesday

CITY JAIL SERVICE
1:30 p.m. -Sunday

CITY STOCKADE SERVICE
3:00 p.m.   Sunday

STREET SERVICE
8:00 p.m.   Monday
(Corner Flagler & Miami Ave.)

RADIO SERVICES
8:15 a.m.   Sunday
WQAM, 560 K.C.

8:00 a.m.
Monday, Wednesday and Friday
WMIE, 1140 K.C.

Annual Report 1957

199,323 free meals provided
73,440 beds provided for men
11 families assisted
4,650 pieces of clothing and shoes
    distributed without charge
120 pieces of furniture given
    without charge
365 gospel services conducted
136 Bible classes for new converts
45 street meetings
51 services in the County Jail
52 services in the City Jail
52 services in the City Stockade
78 radio programs
3,540 confessions of faith in the
    Mission and Jails
320 privately counselled
52 Alcoholics Anonymous meetings
    at Mission.

Bro. and Sister Ash and Son George in front of the little Flagler Street Mission where many souls were blessed for seven busy years before moving in the larger quarters on N.W. First Street.

Front structure of the Mission changed in the 1960's

MIAMI   RESCUE   MISSION

First time the Mission added the signage:
"When you don't have a friend in the
world you'll find one here."

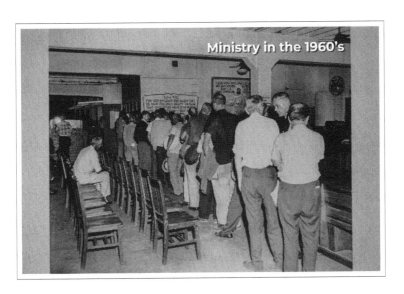

Ministry in the 1960's

Eminent domain occured at 140 NW First Street
and Mission moved to **716 N. Miami Ave.**
(formerly Royal Hotel) in 1979
This is the emergency shelter and
food and clothing center

**MIAMI
RESCUE
MISSION**

716
N. MIAMI AVE.

Site used for one of the *Miami Vice* TV show scenes

Under the Ashes leadership in 1969 this building was built as a "Rehabilitation Work Program for Men" (Men's residential center) Behind this property at 2233 NW 1st Ct was a Thrift Store and Warehouse and Donation Center (Men's work program)

Later became Center for Women & Children in 1989 (at 2250 NW 1st Ave.)

Dr. Frank and Maxine Jacobs

Re-founders of the Mission from 1975 to 2006
Dr. Frank (President) and Maxine Jacobs (Chief Operations Officer)
Under their leadership the Men's Rehabilitation program was reconstructed to be a "Regeneration Program" using the premise of II Corinthians 5:17 "Therefore if any man be in Christ, he is a new creature: old things are passed away; behold, all things are become(ing) new."

1985-1992

Another Thrift Store of the Miami Rescue Mission located in Naranja, Florida.

Interviews for our "Mission Possible" WLRN TV Show

1989-1990

MISSION: POSSIBLE
MIAMI RESCUE MISSION

Miami Homeless in the 80's

Ground Breaking for the Miami Rescue Mission Center for Men (1987)

Dr. Frank Jacobs, Roger Gordon, Mayor Xavier Suarez, Charles Moye, Jeff Tew and Maxine Jacobs

Center for Men Construction (1987-1989)

Miami Rescue Mission
Center for Men

People Queuing for Food while the
building is under construction (1987-1989).
The Chapel would be built later in this spot.

Ribbon Cutting Ceremony for the Center for Men (1989)

Serving annually the Thanksgiving Banquet on the streets

Building transformed from Men's Residential Center to The Center for Women and Children (1989)

Miami Rescue Mission Chapel Service (1989)

Dr. Frank Jacobs talking to the homeless in Chapel (1989)

Jeffrey A. Tew
Education Center
Opened early 1990's

Residents / Students at the
Education Center

Thrift Store Bargain Barn in the 1990's

Pick Up Donation Truck Fleet in the early 1990's

Trucks of the Miami Rescue Mission providing food to the Miami-Dade Community after Hurricane Andrew (1992)

Miami Rescue Mission Administrative Offices (at 2159 NW 1st Ct) (1994)

Ground Breaking for the Broward Outreach Centers (1996)

We were honored with the presence of the Mayor of Hollywood Mara S. Giulianti, (1986 to 2008)

Left to right: Allen Reeser, former BOC Director, Dr. Frank Jacobs, Erica Solodkin, volunteer, Kathleen Anderson, Commissioner, City of Hollywood, Mara Giulianti, former Mayor, City of Hollywood and three other Commissioners.

Police visiting and educating our Center for Women and Children (1990's)

Ronald Brummitt joined staff - (1991)

Ron Brummitt - Teaching Regeneration / Alpha Classes (1990's)

Ron - Graduate of Trinity International University

Broward Outreach Centers
Center for Men purchased and opened in 1997

1997

2022

Jeb Bush
Former Governor of Florida
(early 1990's)
visiting our Center for Men

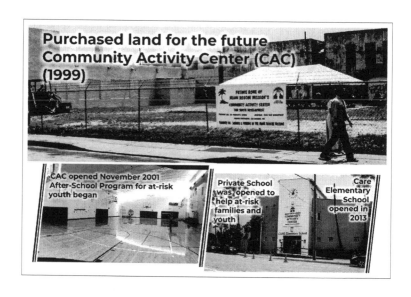

Purchased land for the future Community Activity Center (CAC) (1999)

CAC opened November 2001 After-School Program for at-risk youth began

Private School was opened to help at-risk families and youth

Care Elementary School opened in 2013

Serving Food in the Cafeteria

2004 Rev. Ronald Brummitt
Selected as Executive Director

Board of Directors praying for
Rev. Ron and his wife Marilyn

Ordained For Ministry

Broward Outreach Center
Center for Women
& Children added
in 2005

Center for
Women & Children

Center for Men

Center for Men Annex Building
Adds 78 extra beds plus multipurpose room

Before renovation in 2013

After renovation

Purchased and moved Thrift Store Bargain Barn
(8700 NW 7th Street)
(2016-2022)

Furniture Showroom

Men's Clothing Showroom

Nearly 5 acres of land at 700 NW 175th St., Miami Gardens

The Caring Place Center for Women & Children Future build-out Family Center

Recently dedicated
May 2022

The Caring Place
Dr. Frank & Maxine Jacobs
Center for Men

2022

Rev. Ronald Brummitt
President

Marilyn Brummitt
Wife & VP of Development

PART 3

ANGELS AMONG US

—

Supporters And Donors Of The Miami Rescue Mission

Everyone who gives to the Mission has reasons why, and here are some of their stories

Carole Brock

The Miami Rescue Mission wouldn't exist without its donors, a large collection of incredibly generous individuals who are committed to the cause of helping others.

One of the most inspirational donors is Carole Brock, who was born in Chicago on Oct. 16, 1929. Eight days later, the largest sell-off of stock-market shares in U.S. history happened, triggering the start of the Great Depression.

"I don't know how my father and mother (John and Maria) got through it," Brock said.

Despite the economic hard times, Brock grew up in a happy and spiritual home.

Music was Brock's passion. While her mother was pregnant with her, she would listen to music, and Brock would kick in perfect tune.

Once Brock was born, her mom wanted to buy her child a piano. So, she earned extra cash washing the clothes of her neighbors, and she used that money to buy her daughter a piano. Brock was three years old when she got the piano, and she loved it, even though she didn't know how to play at first.

"I had a few lessons for 25 cents per hour," Brock said. "My mom knew how important music was to me.

"God gave me the talent for music. I used to play piano and sing in church and on cruise ships and at senior centers, in the

U.S. and in England. My music is a gift from God, and it's a gift I still have."

At one point, Brock was part of a singing group called Three's Harmony, with two sisters, Jean and Sally. Brock would also appear on radio and television religious shows, singing and playing the piano.

"My goal was to use my talent to inspire people," Brock said. "It wasn't about singing in bars or night clubs."

In fact, when Brock was 15, her father would drive her – once a month – to a mission in Chicago, where she would play the piano.

"My dad would give me a quarter, and I would donate 10 percent (five cents) to my Sunday School class," Brock said. "I love to give. God has given me this ability to give, and I still donate 10 percent of what I earn, except that I have increased the amounts.

"I believe in giving to charity, and being a child from the Great Depression, every penny, nickel and dime is important."

Growing up, Brock was an excellent student. She was so smart that she skipped a grade twice and graduated from high school at age 17.

From there, she studied to become a secretary, and she was so proficient that she got hired even before she graduated.

At age 25 – tired of the cold weather – Brock moved to Miami.

"God opened so many doors for me," she said. "It was God who has put me in the right place at the right time."

Brock didn't want to get married right away and, in fact, she waited until she was in her 40s.

That's when she met Ken Brock at a high-rise Miami hotel where she was attending a lecture on various topics, including religion and technology.

A friend had invited Brock to the lecture, but he never showed.

"I waited and waited until I heard someone come up the steps," Brock said. "When the man got off the steps, something in me said: 'That's the man I'm going to marry.' This was before he even spoke, and that's what happened.

"Ken sat with me for the lecture, and that's how it started. We had a blessed and beautiful partnership and marriage."

Ken Brock died after nine years of marriage to Carole, who told him she would never marry again.

"He looked at me and said, 'Never say never'," Carole Brock said. "Those were his last words."

After Ken Brock passed away, his best friend, Louis Janos, helped Carole sort out her affairs.

As fate would have it, Carole and Janos became friends and then fell in love. They got married and were happy until he died nine years later.

"I've had two marriages, and that's it," Brock said. "I've learned a lot from those experiences, going through that grief.

"I also lost my sister, Avis May, to coronavirus in 2021. She was like a twin to me."

Besides the substantial sorrow associated with those losses,

Brock – who never had children -- said she is content and happy.

"I never expected to get married even once," she said. "I was alone, but I wasn't alone because God was with me.

"God is my purpose. God is real. He is with us. He has the blueprint. God's way is the best way."

Brock, who worked for 30 years for the City of Miami transportation department as an executive assistant, retired in 1986.

"I retired for my spiritual vocation, which is music and also giving to charities such as the Miami Rescue Mission," Brock said. "I'm going to keep giving until I pass away. And even after I die, I will still give because it's in my will."

Edward and Cathi O'Brien

Edward O'Brien and his wife Cathi – both from the greater Philadelphia area – are also strong supporters of the mission.

They moved to Miami in 1995. One year later, Edward decided to donate his 20-foot boat – which was in need of repair – to the mission.

Six months after making the donation, O'Brien got a call notifying him that someone at the mission who was handy with tools had fixed the boat.

"They sold it for $7,000, and that excited me," said O'Brien, who worked for more than 30 years in human-resources management for several large companies. "It caused me to look into the mission more, and we have been giving to the mission ever since."

In 2014, O'Brien and his wife went to the mission's Miami campus to attend a graduation ceremony. They witnessed more than 100 formerly homeless men graduate from the mission's program.

"We were very impressed," O'Brien said. "We spoke to about 20 young graduates. We saw their housing, where they eat their meals and where they get their education and training.

"They were so appreciative. They wanted to talk about the Lord.

"The people at the mission do great work. They are humble servants. Almost all the money they get goes to services for the homeless because they don't spend on marketing or advertising.

"I love that they help the downtrodden. They educate them and help them find and rebuild their self-esteem, and they do it all through the Lord."

On occasions, O'Brien and his wife have helped the homeless on Sundays after church, working in the kitchen.

"We did that for two years, and it makes you feel blessed that you are helping others," O'Brien said.

"The Lord expects us to help others. The Book of James said: 'The religion that is true and honorable helps the poor, the widows and the children', and 90 percent of our charitable giving goes to those types of causes.

"We believe Jesus Christ is our Lord and savior and that the Holy Spirit guides us. God has taken care of us and expects us to care for others."

Roland Malins-Smith

Homelessness and hunger are huge problems that can be discouraging to anyone with a heart.

But Grenada native Roland Malins-Smith, who has been donating to the mission for more than 30 years, takes a different view.

"If you save even one life, it is very valuable," said Malins-Smith, who retired from the business world in 2017. "The mission has salvaged the lives of thousands of people. They do valuable work in the community."

Malins-Smith sold his "Sea Freight" shipping-container business in 2015, which has opened up more time for his charitable work.

A successful businessman, Malins-Smith came to the U.S. in 1980, and he quickly found the Miami Rescue Mission.

"Homelessness is something that touches the heart," Malins-Smith said.

Malins-Smith was so committed to good causes that he took his only daughter, Alana, to the mission when she was 12 years old so she could learn about it and ultimately do a school project on the subject.

Now married, Alana Kaplan is still involved in charity work as a volunteer for the mission's Broward Outreach Center.

"We lead privileged lives," Malins-Smith said of Americans in general. "When you compare our circumstances to those folks who are living on the street ... They need material help. They need protection from the elements. They often need psychological help.

"There is a huge division in this country between the 'haves and halve-nots'. Poverty is an issue which doesn't receive enough attention from politicians."

Malins-Smith appreciates that the mission combines spiritual healing with material outreach.

"One can spend on food and housing," Malins-Smith said. "But you cannot neglect the spiritual side of the person.

"That is what the mission does so well. It renews hope and faith."

Guy Edson

When long-time swimming coach Guy Edson examined his life a couple of decades ago, something didn't quite add up.

Community service was on his list of 10 core values, but he didn't feel like he was living up to his ideals.

At times, he would volunteer with Habitat for Humanity, but it was a scatter-shot approach to community service. He wasn't making as big an impact as he would like, and his commitment to service lacked direction.

"I would ask myself, 'What are you doing about community service?'" said Edson, a former swimmer who made it to nationals in 1973 while competing for Syracuse University. "And the answer was really nothing. I didn't think I was living the life I defined."

That changed one day at church, where he read a bulletin announcement that they were looking for volunteer teachers at the Broward Outreach Center.

Edson seized the opportunity and taught life skills and personal management at that Pompano Beach location for 15 years. He taught one hour once per week (usually Tuesdays or Wednesdays).

"I just loved it," Edson said of his time spent teaching at the mission. "It was the best part of my week.

"I'd spend hours of my free time thinking about what I wanted to talk about. Through the years, I came up with about

40 topics. They were all connected, but there were different approaches."

Edson taught a wide range of people – men and women, young and old.

"Everything I thought I knew about homelessness was thrown out the window," said Edson, a native of Union Center in upstate New York. "Every culture that you can imagine was represented. They all had stories of how they got there, and it was always hard to hear."

Edson was particularly struck when one day – while teaching his class at the Broward Outreach Center – he was greeted by a former swimmer he used to coach.

"He came up to me and said, 'Hi Coach, it's Nathan'," Edson said. "He was a young man who had a difficult time with success.

"Whenever he got a job promotion, he would fall off the wagon and start drinking again. He would freak out. He didn't want or couldn't handle added responsibility."

Edson said his experience doing his volunteer work is that the majority of homeless people he has encountered have suffered through addiction to drugs and/or alcohol. Some, he said, have a mental illness.

"The number of people who became homeless due strictly to economic reasons without addiction or mental illness is relatively small," Edson said. "The hardest cases to stomach are the women and children who become homeless to escape domestic abuse."

Edson had to stop teaching his Pompano Beach class when his coaching career got too involved, especially with a frequent amounts of international travel.

For example, Edson has coached swim clinics in 26 countries.

However, since retiring in 2020, Edson has new-found time to volunteer and has made a commitment to return to the mission.

In addition to teaching a class, Edson plans on going a big step further and serving as a mentor to students.

"It will be similar to how Alcoholics Anonymous has sponsors," Edson said.

Meanwhile, Carol, who is Edson's wife, will also be involved. She is a physical therapist and will teach a functional fitness class, making it a family affair.

"Volunteering at the mission fulfills a need to help others," Edson said. "To serve God is to serve others.

"Some people keep waiting for God to perform miracles. But God performs miracles through people. We all have different talents and purposes. God gives us gifts and the purpose is to share those gifts with other people."

The Elegant Family

Miami Dade College professor Jennifer Elegant was teaching her "Psychology of Personal Effectiveness" course when her world got rocked.

As part of her class, Elegant's students often shared stories from their lives. But on this particular day, one student blew Elegant's mind with his tale of addiction and ultimate redemption.

"This was back in 2008," Elegant said. "I was teaching my 'how to be successful and happy in life' class. It's a great class. Studies have shown that students are far more likely to graduate from MDC if they take that course.

"My students tend to be fabulous. Many of them work multiple jobs. But this one student, Richard – he stood out. He told his story of overcoming addiction, and he was very inspiring to the rest of my students. I felt like he could actually teach the 'how to be happy' class.

"So, I asked him, 'How did you get here? How did you get to be so strong?'

"He told us about the Miami Rescue Mission and how they saved him and were actually paying for his education at MDC.

"When he said that, I got chills."

Elegant went home that night and told her husband, Justin, a high-powered attorney, what she had discovered about the Miami Rescue Mission.

Justin was similarly amazed, and, that very year, the Elegant family – including sons Luke and Hudson, who were 8 and 6 years old at the time – went to the mission to help serve Thanksgiving meals to the residents.

The entire Elegant family was incredibly impressed with what they witnessed at the mission.

"I know a lot of charities that feed people experiencing homelessness," Jennifer Elegant said. "But to me, that is a band-aid.

"The Miami Rescue Mission does so much more than feed people."

As Elegant found out, the mission helps residents get their GEDs. They help them get a college education. They provide job training. They help them with their resumes. They train them on computers. They teach them English if that is required. They provide housing and tend to their medical needs, both physical and psychological.

Ever since that first exposure, the Elegant family has become more and more involved with the mission each year.

"I was shocked that the mission does so much," Jennifer Elegant said. "I didn't know about them or what they do, and my friends didn't know, either.

"But once I found them, I wanted to spread the word. The mission became part of the fabric of our lives and all our friends' lives."

In fact, Luke – who is now an Ivy League student and an aspiring lawyer at the University of Pennsylvania – and his brother helped modernize the mission's fundraising efforts.

"Initially, we worked with 'Go Fund Me'," Luke said. "But as a third-party platform, they take a seven-percent cut, which is a lot.

"So, we helped to create a link on the Miami Rescue Mission website so that there is no middle man. There is no tax. You can just click and donate. From our original idea, most of the donors now have their own pages on the Miami Rescue Mission site."

To date, Luke and his brother have raised an impressive amount of money for the mission -- $65,000.

"When I first started going to the mission at eight years old, I didn't understand everything, but I knew we were doing a good thing," Luke said. "By age 13, I wanted to take on more of a leadership role.

"Every year since, my brother and I have been team captains of the annual Thanksgiving lunch."

Beyond the fundraising, Luke and Hudson have tutored residents of the mission, helping them get their GEDs.

While doing his tutoring work, Luke said he has heard inspiring stories from residents who were formerly incarcerated. Some were military veterans. Others were simply trying to learn a trade so that they could support their families.

"I met one man who told me he would never be able to learn math," Luke said. "At the end, he got a score of 90 percent. He looked at me and he said: 'I couldn't have done this without you.'

"I said, 'You did all the work.' Then I was able to join him at his graduating ceremony."

Luke said he is proud to help.

"I'm so happy I'm able to make a difference in someone's life," he said. "Being able to make a difference even on a micro level is awesome. I've learned a lot about real life and the world and myself."

When the COVID-19 pandemic hit in 2020, Luke and Hudson started a "From The Heart" initiative in which elementary-school kids write letters of support to residents of the Miami Rescue Mission.

It's enough to make your heart melt.

"We wanted the residents to know that even during COVID – when it's harder for people to volunteer in person – they are still not alone," Luke said.

The Elegant family involvement extends beyond Jennifer, Justin, Luke and Hudson. Jennifer said her father-in-law, Ira Elegant, who passed away recently, was a very generous Miami Rescue Mission donor.

In addition, Jennifer's father, Joel Channing, is a significant presence at Miami Rescue Mission events.

"He plays chess or checkers with the residents," Jennifer said. "He eats with them.

"A big piece in all of this is connecting with people, making eye contact, smiling. People who are experiencing homelessness are often made to feel invisible, alone, unheard, unseen and unimportant, and one way to connect is to play games."

Jennifer said "it feels so good" to be able to help others.

"I'm not a big fan of sending money to a charity and not knowing what your money does," Elegant said. "That's why I'm so grateful to the Miami Rescue Mission. I know the money we send is literally saving and changing lives."

Marilyn Brummitt

All of her early training – in Christian faith, business, teaching and more – has come full circle in the role of a lifetime

Back in 1950 in Columbus, Ohio, Evelyn and Martin Sharp had a baby girl named Marilyn. They didn't know it at the time, but God – from the very beginning – was preparing Marilyn for something truly special.

Marilyn is now the Vice President of Development at the Miami Rescue Mission, a job in which she incorporates so much of what she has learned over the decades – business, teaching, public speaking, computer skills, financial planning and, of course, a love for the Lord.

"I see the hand of God through everything that's happened," Marilyn said.

Because of her allergies, Marilyn's parents moved the family to Venice, Florida when she was just five years old.

At age 10, one of Marilyn's teachers asked her to draw a picture of what she wanted to do when she got older. Marilyn drew herself standing with a bunch of children around her and a caption that read:

"Missionary to Africa."

Marilyn remembers her teacher laughing as she read that caption in front of the class.

"I asked my mom: 'Why did she think that was funny?' I was hurt," Marilyn said. "That teacher made the kids laugh at me, but it didn't deter me from my goal.

"At my church at that time, our pastor would introduce us to missionaries who would return from trips to places such as Africa or countries in Asia. The missionaries would show slides of the people they met, and it would make me cry. I would tell my mom: 'I want to go tell those people about Jesus'."

Growing up, Marilyn's father, Martin, was an entrepreneur, a builder and a self-taught architect, and both her parents were deeply committed to the Lord and the Baptist church.

Initially, the family business was a shopping center – built by Martin -- called Springs Plaza, which was located in Warm Mineral Springs, Florida.

"My dad was self-taught at everything," Marilyn said. "He loved electronics. It was a subject he would read about and then do projects.

"One day, a neighbor had a television set that was broken. The neighbor told my dad: 'If you can fix it, great, but, if not, throw it away.'

"My dad took it as a challenge and fixed it, charging the guy $12. The guy was so happy that he told all the neighbors. All of a sudden, the back room of our house was full of neighbors' TV sets that were waiting for my dad to fix."

Marilyn's mom wasn't pleased.

"She said: 'You need to get all these TVs out of the house. I want my room back.'

"So, my dad opened up a tiny TV shop, using a quarter of the space he had been trying to rent for one of the stores at the shopping center.

"After that, he started also selling new television sets. His business was called: 'Springs TV and Appliance'."

Meanwhile, Marilyn had graduated from Venice High School and had gotten through one year of Miami Bible College, which later became Trinity International University.

She had intended to do three more years of Bible study before going into some kind of ministry work, but God had another idea. Remember, God was preparing her for the role of a lifetime, but she didn't or couldn't fully know that at the time.

What she did know was the immediate circumstances, which involved a massive robbery of her father's business. Martin had just accepted delivery of about 30 TVs, and, the next morning, they were gone.

Martin had no insurance, and the theft of the entire contents of his store almost put him out of business.

Marilyn, just 19 years old at the time, left Miami Bible College to help her father. After all, she had worked in the store part-time while she had gone to high school.

Martin, who hated owing money, had no choice but to take out a bank loan to keep the business afloat.

"That loan took years to pay off," Marilyn said. "I started working at the store full-time because my dad couldn't afford to hire help at that time. My parents needed me."

Even so, Marilyn's grandparents didn't want her to just work in the store. They figured that would not be enough to further whatever career path she would take in the future.

So, her grandparents lovingly paid for Marilyn to go to a vocational school to learn computers, and that would prove to be highly beneficial.

Leaving Miami Bible College was a period of great consternation for Marilyn and her family. Marilyn's mother, Evelyn, had wanted her to stay in school. But Marilyn's father wanted her to help the family business.

"My mom had graduated from Ohio State and, initially, she was a registered nurse," Marilyn said. "Later, she taught herself book-keeping to help my dad.

"On the side, my mom was a great Bible teacher. She would open our home and invite the neighbors. She would often have 10 to 15 women in the house for Bible study. It didn't matter if those women went to church or not. It didn't matter their religion. They just loved to hear her teach."

Marilyn inherited her mom's gift for teaching and her father's knack for business. She helped save the family business, and she started studying computers in 1971.

Soon, however, there would be another major change in her life.

It was at her computer class that she met a young man, Siegfried "Ziggy" Pitambersingh, who was from Suriname. Ziggy, was brought up in a Muslim family, got the name Siegfried because he was delivered by a German doctor. As the story goes, that doctor said:

"I've delivered so many of this family's babies, aand now I have delivered twins, I want to name them Siegfried and Wilfred."

Ziggy, who had a Dutch passport and had many family members living in Holland, worked for Texaco but came to the U.S. specifically to study computers.

"He later told me the first time he noticed me was in the break room of our computer class," Marilyn said. "All these young people were talking about their weekend, and they turned to me and asked what I did, and I said, 'I went to church, and I taught a Sunday School class for children.'

"They made fun of me. They said, 'All this girl cares about is church and Jesus.'

"But (Ziggy) heard me talking, and he thought, 'I want to get to know her.' He really took an interest in me, and I had never experienced that genuine interest from a guy before and he was very interested in knowing more about the Bible and Jesus. We had great conversations. He started going to church with me."

Marilyn said that, given her and Ziggy's racial, ethnic and religious differences in up-bringing, she did meet resistance from her family.

"My grandfather wrote me a letter that said, "Bluebirds marry bluebirds. Redbirds marry redbirds,' Marilyn said.

"But I was so madly in love – there was nothing else I could do. This was a love story, head over heels. It didn't matter what others thought.

""He was kind, funny and had a genuine interest in learning more about Jesus. He loved me, and he showed it."

Marilyn said her family ultimately accepted and loved Ziggy. The young couple married in 1972, and they soon moved to Holland. Their first of two children, Joy Endira, was born in Holland, but moving there was a bit of culture shock for Marilyn.

Her husband's family spoke four different languages – seemingly all at the same time.

"It took me one year just to differentiate the four languages," Marilyn said. "The main language was Dutch, but they also spoke Hindustani and a dialect of Surinam and English as well (at least the brothers and sisters did). My mother-in-law did not.

"I also learned a lot about Indian foods."

Marilyn said marrying her husband made her aware of the world and an existence outside her own upbringing.

"I've always believed all people are one race but just with different ethnicities," Marilyn said. "Marrying Ziggy opened my eyes to different cultures."

"His family loved on me," Marilyn said. "It started out as missionary dating, but changed into real love." Ziggy would ask me questions about what I believed. He eventually accepted the Lord Jesus as his savior and was baptized in America.

"That could've cost problems with his family. But they were a westernized, modern family. I remember praying with his mother. They loved me, and I loved them."

While living in Europe, Marilyn used to carry a Dutch-to-English dictionary. She finally learned the language by taking night classes and also speaking with children.

"It was hard at first," Marilyn said, "but children speak in an elementary way, and it was easier to communicate with them."

Marilyn and her husband both worked in a Dutch computer lab. The company then sent her to school in Amsterdam to learn computer programming, which brought the young family back to Florida in 1976. By then, Marilyn's parents' TV business had grown, and they wanted someone who could repair appliances.

Seeing the opportunity, Ziggy traveled to Ann Arbor, Michigan for two weeks. He attended what was known as Whirlpool School, and he learned about the appliance business.

In 1977, Marilyn and her husband had a son, Mark Siegfried, and, by the early 1980s, microwaves had hit the market. Marilyn started to experiment, learning how to cook with her microwave, and that's when her business instincts started to kick into gear.

For almost the entire decade of the 1980s, she owned and operated "Marilyn's Microwave" in Port Charlotte, Florida.

Marilyn and Ziggy made a good team, with her "'Type A" personality and his comfort in letting her run the proverbial show.

"He loved me so much that he allowed me to take control," Marilyn said. "I loved him so much that I knew when to acquiesce.

"For our Marilyn's Microwave company, I was doing advertising and sales. I was the face of the business, but he was the guy behind the scenes. He kept the customers happy and did all the stuff I didn't want to do."

Ever the entrepreneur, Marilyn held cooking classes in her store, teaching women how to cook with this new-fangled microwave. She taught those classes four times a week, and it helped her sell a ton of microwaves.

"If they bought a microwave, I would only charge them a nominal fee for the class," Marilyn said. "I taught a beginner's class, a holiday class and an advanced class.

"I had people on a waiting list for the classes. I hit the wave at the right time. During Christmas season, I would sell 70 microwaves a day.

"For a little business, it was phenomenal."

Marilyn soon started making TV and radio advertisements for her store, and that would be yet another skill that would come in handy in her later years.

"My kids helped me make our TV ads," Marilyn said.

By this point, Marilyn's father had retired, and she was running his business as well as her own. Marilyn had 10 people working for her between the two stores.

Her husband had become known in their North Port, Florida community as a youth-soccer coach, but, otherwise, he had to make the adjustment to the U.S.

"When we were living in Europe, I was the odd one," Marilyn said. "But when we returned to Florida, (Ziggy) was the odd one in a way. But he was so personable that everyone loved him, and I mean everyone.

"We brought up our kids to never feel there is a difference in races. My kids have darker skin and dark hair, and I'm white with blonde hair. Our kids loved their father and their family on both sides. It was a rich recipe of cultures and good food."

For their first 13 years as a family in Florida, Marilyn, Ziggy and the kids lived in a tiny, 800-square-foot house.

Finally, in January of 1990, they moved to a spacious and impressive two-story house – 3,600 square feet.

In August of that year, Ziggy turned 50 years old, and his twin brother, Wilfred, helped throw him a big party.

Then in October – still active in his favorite sport – Ziggy played a terrific club soccer game.

"He scored from midfield, and he was thrilled," Marilyn said. "He said, 'The old man still has it. I may not have the same endurance, but I've still got the power'."

After the game, he came home. He ate some food, and he went to lay down. However, he told Marilyn he was in pain.

"He said, 'You need to take me to the hospital right now'," said Marilyn, relaying the conversation. "We had been married 18 years at that time, and he had never said anything like that before."

Ziggy was in the hospital for two weeks. Doctors were prepping him for a quintuple bypass.

"I knew it was an important surgery, but I didn't expect him to die," Marilyn said. "Before the surgery, I said, 'I love you,' and that's the last thing I ever said to him."

After the quintuple bypass, Marilyn waited for hours at the hospital, hoping for good news.

"Finally, I got upset," Marilyn said. "I told them, 'I'm going to go through those doors if you don't let me see my husband.'

"The doctor finally came out and said the operation was a success, but (Ziggy) had another heart attack between the operating room and the recovery room.

"I never talked to him again. He could squeeze my hand a little bit, but he was never fully conscious again. It was a huge blow for me."

That's actually an understatement.

Marilyn, who was 40 when her husband passed away, spent the next two years in a deep depression, feeling alone in her big, new house.

"I was probably clinically depressed, even though I didn't seek out a diagnosis," Marilyn said. "I had been so dependent, emotionally, on my husband. When I lost him, I had to re-evaluate just about everything I had believed."

Ziggy's death had an impact that went beyond Marilyn. It hit their kids, too.

"Both of my children suffered with the loss of their dad. My daughter and I had a hard time communicating and no longer lived at home. My son, was home but there was too much emotional pain for me to connect to him correctly. I couldn't connect with my children because I didn't even know who I was anymore".

Just before Ziggy died, Marilyn – ever the entrepreneur – was in the process of changing her career plan yet again. From Bible college student to business owner and now . . . financial planning.

She was working at City Financial and was on her way to becoming a financial planner (she was working on her CFP at the time).

"Our family had always known about real estate," Marilyn

said. "But I didn't know anything about investing money. I was good at making financial budgets, but I didn't know the difference between a stock and a bond."

While Marilyn worked on a career change, something incredible happened. About five weeks before Ziggy died, Marilyn said she had an "encounter" with God.

"It's the only time I felt I audibly heard from God," Marilyn said. "I was on 1-75, driving home from my financial job in Sarasota. God spoke to me while I was in the car. He said: 'Marilyn, I want you back in the church.'"

Hearing God's voice must have been shocking, but the timing was also off for Marilyn.

She was on her way to becoming somebody in the financial world. Disappointed with church politics, she had also stopped attending services.

"I was a weaker Christian at that time," she said. "Some things had happened, and I had decided to worship from home, even though the Bible says do not forsake the assembling of yourselves together."

Given that decision to worship from home, Marilyn said she talked back to God that day in the car.

"I was rebellious," she said. "I said, 'Really? Where do you want me to go? I'm not going to any of those dead churches.'

"I felt like I hadn't been growing anymore. But I also realized that I had focused on the politics that I didn't like instead of focusing on God."

After her bit of rebellious attitude that day in the car, Marilyn said God responded.

"God immediately told me: 'I want you to go to the church on Center Road.'"

This was another request Marilyn found difficult. The church on Center Road was Pentecostal. Marilyn had been raised Baptist.

In her mind, the Pentecostal church members were way more emotional than she was comfortable with in her worship of the Lord.

She had visited a Pentecostal church once with her daughter. After the service had ended, Marilyn and her daughter both thought the same thing: All that clapping and hand-raising wasn't for them.

So, for God to ask her to go to that specific church was a bit of a tough ask.

That next Sunday, however, Marilyn was there, at the church on Center Road, with her young son.

Then, when her husband died, Marilyn could barely get out of bed that first year. She managed to continue to go to that church on Center Road, however, but she was not an active participant in the services.

"I was like a dead stick," Marilyn said. "I just stood there. I didn't talk to a lot of people.

"But there was an assistant pastor there who would bring me food during the days I was depressed. She would call me every once in a while, but it seemed like she would appear when I really needed her, when I was in my deepest depression."

Although she was back in the church, mending her broken

heart was anything but a quick fix. The first six years following Ziggy's death was a period of wandering and soul-searching. She existed -- but barely.

There was no joy in her life.

In 1992, two years after Ziggy died, Marilyn earned a certified financial planning license. In 1994, she earned a Bachelor of Arts degree from Edison Community College. Her major was business administration.

Those were notable achievements, especially considering her grief.

But, again, no joy.

"I remember sitting in class and being so sad," Marilyn said. "All these college students ... This should be a happy time.

"But I wasn't happy. Everything was an effort. It was hard to get up in the morning. I had a difficult time wanting to do anything. I just forced myself."

During those days, weeks and months of depression, Marilyn searched for answers. She read the Koran, for example. She studied other religions. She learned about philosophy.

"I wanted to fully know what the choices were," Marilyn said. "One day, I got down on my knees. I said: 'Lord, is there a hope of knowing you and having an understanding that there is more to life than just here. Is there eternity?'

"Eventually, I said to God: 'I am making a choice, whether or not anyone can prove to me it's real. I choose you. I'm totally in your hands. I totally surrender.'

"But I also said: 'God, I have nothing to give you. All my

self-esteem is gone. My love of life is gone. I don't feel like teaching anymore. I don't have anything to give.'"

Marilyn said she didn't hear an audible response from the Lord, but the message was equally clear.

Jesus was whispering a gentle reminder that because I had nothing to give that all would come from Him and that I would know in the future that I was not the one to rebuild myself, it would be all Him. Marilyn didn't know it at the time, but other lost souls would present themselves in her life, and God could use her to help them heal.

Still, worship in a Pentecostal church was something Marilyn went into with a great deal of trepidation. At first, she found the clapping and hand-raising "weird".

But, one Sunday at her church on Center Road, Marilyn heard the choir sing:

"I don't worship You (Lord) for what you have done," they sang. "I worship You (Lord) for who you are."

When Marilyn heard those words, she started to weep.

"Oh Lord, that's me." she thought. "I only praise you when things are good.

"I started to understand that worship was part of our reason for being here on Earth. It's about praising God for who He is and not for what he gives or does not give."

Marilyn said the Pentecostal church has helped bring the joy back to her life.

"Prior to this, I knew the mechanics of the Bible – the verses, the Old and New Testament. I knew all that stuff,"

Marilyn said. "But now God was leading me to understand who He is, understanding that God is supreme and that he loves us."

Part of Marilyn's recovery came when she started teaching Sunday School again. This brought out her creative side as she searched for ways to keep the children engaged.

That started Marilyn on another journey. She asked God for direction. She said God told her to write her resume all over again with more of a focus on her spiritual side instead of her financial planning. So, she did just that, including her mission trips and Sunday School teaching.

"I was learning to do what God told me," Marilyn said. "If you can't hear God's voice, how can you follow Him?"

Armed with this new direction, Marilyn went to her pastor Rev. Gary Gray and showed him her resume.

He immediately led her to what was, essentially, an oversized closet.

This was her tiny new office, complete with a desk, a door and a key.

The pastor then invited her to sit in on staff meetings. He wanted her to be church's education director.

"God said to me: 'Now you can use your financial background. There are people who can't afford to pay their light bills, and you can help them.'

"I ended up teaching a class for parishioners who needed help with budgeting."

In 2000 — 10 years after the death of her husband–she started talking to Ron Brummitt, who at that time was the director of the Miami Rescue Mission's Miami campus.

Marilyn was introduced to the Miami Rescue Mission by an old friend she and her husband knew when they lived in Holland. That friend convinced her to eventually take a tour of the Miami Center, which is where she first met Brummitt.

"Between 1994 and 2000, Ron and I knew of each other, but it was no big deal," Marilyn said. "My friend who had introduced us talked to me about how Ron had a heart for people."

"I saw Ron like I saw everyone else who was around at the time. These were people in the ministry, and I would do anything I could to help people in the ministry."

In 2000, when Marilyn came back from a mission trip to Thailand, her pastor called on her to help with some counseling on a case that had to do with immigration.

"I didn't know how to help these people," Marilyn said. "I called Ron for advice, and we started talking professionally."

From counseling to help with her computer, Brummitt continued to make himself useful, although Marilyn still thought of the relationship as a friendship and not a budding romance.

In November of 2000, Marilyn's missionary friend, Audrey, needed her help to drive a van to Miami. The van was loaded with clothes, canned foods and other essential items that were going to be shipped to the poor in Haiti.

Audrey and Marilyn had traveled about 10 times on mission trips to Haiti and Jamaica.

On this trip to Miami, Marilyn reached out to Brummitt for logistical help.

Brummitt said yes to the call for help. He and Marilyn

drove the lead car down to Miami, with the van following. Upon arrival, Marilyn would take the car back home while Brummitt stayed in Miami.

But something magical happened on that car trip. While crossing Alligator Alley, Marilyn realized how nice it was to have a friend who shared her passion to help the less fortunate. It was nice to make one phone call to that same friend and – voila – he had the entire trip mapped out. Everything was handled.

Marilyn and Brummitt started out on that car trip at about 4:30 in the morning. Marilyn brought her pillow, thinking she would sleep while Brummitt drove, but they ended up talking … and talking … and talking.

Brummitt finally asked her: "Is there something else happening here between us?"

Said Marilyn: "I knew what he meant, but I was petrified. I said: 'Maybe'."

Even a response as tenuous as "maybe" changed everything. The rest of the car trip was spent with both Brummitt and Marilyn sharing their opinions on various topics.

By February of 2001, Brummitt had been asked to travel to Israel by a volunteer worker at the mission. Brummitt, who had always dreamed of traveling to Israel, served as sort of a bodyguard and travel companion.

But, while in Israel, Brummitt filmed himself telling Marilyn that he loved her, using the Dead Sea as the backdrop.

When Brummitt returned home, he showed Marilyn the video.

At that point, Brummitt asked Marilyn: "You counsel a lot of people. What would you advise to two people who want to remarry?"

Marilyn said: "I would tell them to wait one year to make sure it's real love and not a rash decision."

Brummitt said: "Shucks, I would say the same thing."

For Marilyn to wait an entire year seemed like a big ask.

"I was head over heels in love again," she said. "I never thought I would feel like that again."

Brummitt officially asked her to marry him in July of 2001. They married on Feb. 16, 2002.

"The reason I love Ron so much is that he has a compassion that is almost supernatural," Marilyn said. "When the City of North Port dedicated a soccer field in honor of Ziggy (Marilyn's first husband that had died). Ron went there with me and filmed the whole thing. Ron also went back through all the old tapes (of Ziggy), and he made a beautiful video in his honor."

Once she had re-married, Marilyn knew Brummitt's job was too important to give up, and it was up to her to make the move down to Miami.

"I was a director at our church. I did have an important position," she said. "But Ron had a more important position at a much larger ministry. We didn't talk about the move that was needed, but he knew, and I knew."

Marilyn also knew that she would have to apply for a job at the Miami Rescue Mission as opposed to anything being handed to her.

Marilyn had an interest in the women's center. Homelessness among women was a growing problem.

She wanted to know if she could live at the women's center for one week so that she could know what the issues were and how best to solve them.

This request was unheard of, but Brummitt made it happen.

"I stayed in a room just like a homeless woman," Marilyn said. "I ate with the women. I showered there. I helped in the kitchen. I did everything they did.

"When I came home on Saturday and then went to church on Sunday, something came over me. At church, I couldn't move. I could not drive home. I was overcome with the spirit of God in a way I had never felt.

"A friend drove me home, a Godly woman. I told her what I had done the past week.

"She said: 'You are being overwhelmed by the Holy Spirit. You have been impacted by these women and what they go through on a daily basis.'

"It wasn't sympathy. It was empathy. I felt it – their pain became my pain."

Marilyn wanted to work with these women and their children. But, unfortunately, there were no openings at the time.

The only opening was for a volunteer coordinator. Marilyn wasn't sure exactly what that was except that it sounded a whole lot like what she had done at her previous church.

She got the job, and she soon discovered that being a volunteer coordinator would allow her to see how the entire ministry works.

Marilyn said the Miami Rescue Mission doesn't force religion on anyone. They are shown God's love in practical ways.

"But even before introducing them to the Lord and letting them make that choice, we know that people can't be taught about God if they are hungry or unclean," Marilyn said.

"Everything is done to show them that God loves them. God has a purpose for each life."

Marilyn has certainly found her purpose. As the Miami Rescue Mission's Vice President of Development, she is a fundraiser as well as a friend-raiser.

People give of their time, talent and treasure because they are engaged in the mission, and Marilyn is a big part of that effort.

In addition, she is a mom to Joy and Mark and an eight-time grandmother. Joy lives in North Port, Florida. Mark lives in Edmond, Oklahoma.

Along the way, Marilyn has accomplished so much at the mission, teaching financial budgeting, computer skills and Bible studies. She also contributes to the mission's several weekly radio shows, something she would never have dreamed of when she had a fear of public speaking as a young girl.

"You always want to empower people to be successful," Marilyn said. "When I rededicated my life to Jesus, I began to see God's hand in everything. God remade me, and I began to give God the glory in all things.

"It's funny because as a 10-year-old girl I wanted to be a missionary. I failed to fulfill that goal. But only God can give you a second chance like He has given me. All along, God was preparing me for what was to come.

"I didn't see the big picture earlier in my life. I didn't know God's plan. What I didn't understand for the longest time was the 'how'. I knew I didn't have time at this point in my life to go back to Bible college.

"So, God brought me here to marry Ron. Yes, I fell in love, but I was really marrying the mission as well as Ron. God brought a whole world of ministry to my door."

PART 4

A NEW DAY

—

From growing the Miami Rescue Mission
to becoming The Caring Place, the future is
bright for the next 100 years

While the first 50 years of the mission featured numerous struggles, the past half-century has been a period of incredible growth.

The mission has become one of the nation's largest providers of life-saving and essential services for the homeless, the hungry, the abused and the needy, including displaced men, women and children.

A non-profit organization, the mission is a charitable, faith-based agency that provides spiritual, physical and social services. The goal is to transform lives through comprehensive programs. These programs help create lasting change, empowering people to become productive members of society.

The Caring Place, aka the Miami Rescue Mission, provides food, shelter, clothing, treatment for substance abuse, education, computer literacy, job placement, health care, spiritual development and housing. All of that is accomplished through compassion, encouragement and Christian love.

Homelessness is defined as lacking a regular and adequate night-time residence, and the Miami Rescue Mission is addressing this problem that – sadly – is growing.

In 2020, according to the Department of Housing and Urban Development, 580,466 people experienced homelessness in the U.S. on any given night. That was the fourth year in a row that the number went up, and the 2021 count was believed to be skewed due to COVID-19. California, for example, did not take a count of its unsheltered population in 2021, due to the pandemic.

Still, the HUD study shows some disturbing trends:

= There are 171,670 families with children reporting as homeless as of 2020. Not since the Great Depression have there been so many homeless families. In the 1980s, for example, families accounted for less than 1 percent of those experiencing homelessness. Today, families account for a stunning 30 percent of the homeless population.

= Of the 580,446 people counted as homeless, 354,386 are sheltered and more than 226,000 are unsheltered.

= Of the total count of those experiencing homelessness, 34,210 (or about six percent) are unaccompanied youth under the age of 25. Roughly half of them are living in unsheltered environments.

= More than 39 percent of the people experiencing homelessness are women. And 84 percent of those women have suffered severe physical and/or sexual abuse at some point in their lives.

= Despite major strides made over the past decade, there are 37,252 (or about eight percent) homeless veterans.

= There are 120,323 people (or about 20 percent) classified as chronically homeless. That means they have been homeless for more than one year, and they have had multiple periods of homelessness over the previous three years. The majority of those who are chronically homeless – about 54 percent – are unsheltered.

= According to a separate report, this one from July of 2020, Blacks – who comprise 13 percent of the American population -- account for 40 percent of the overall homelessness count.

Education is a key component to the homeless issue. An estimated 53 percent of the homeless population have less than a high school education. Other causes of homelessness include substance abuse, domestic violence, mental-health issues and either unemployment or low-paying jobs.

Locally, the Miami Rescue Mission had for decades focused on the inner city. But in 1992, the mission branched out and started serving in Broward County. The mission opened the Broward Outreach Center (BOC) in Hollywood in 1997. BOC was the first to provide both emergency shelter and comprehensive recovery programs for the homeless in the southern portion of Broward.

In 2002, two locations in Broward were in operation. The Hollywood Center held up to 147 men, women and children. The Pompano Center had room for 220 men, women and children, and the average length of stay is anywhere from 90 days to six months. In 2005 Broward Outreach Center in Hollywood opened a 4 story building for women and children.

The mission served in Pompano Beach on Blount Road for 18 years operating the county facilities. In 2019 the county no longer needed those services. The Broward Outreach Centers in Hollywood have made the Big, Bold decision in 2022 to include the Regeneration Discipleship program in like manner as the Miami Campus. The real transformation comes with people finding how much God loves them and finding purpose through his love.

Beyond the Broward Outreach Center, 1997 was also

the year the Miami Rescue Mission opened the Jeffrey A. Tew Adult Education and Career Center. A part of the Tew Center's objective is to teach those who are illiterate to read and write. Others are put on the path toward earning their high school equivalency (GED). The program focuses on adult education through computer competency, and it even includes a memory-therapy program for those who have suffered memory loss.

The students who successfully complete the educational requirements move on to Career Employment Services, where the main focus is a development of job-search skills. The key for those in the CES program is the ability to adjust in order to find jobs and careers in the work-force market.

Many students in the program go on to college or acquire specialized training in a variety of fields, including hospitality, food service or trucking.

Meanwhile, in Miami-Dade County, there are two residential centers.

There's the Center for Men, which provides 260 beds, including transitional housing and long-term residential care. On average, there are about 140 men per day involved in the 12-to-24-month intensive program, which provides counseling, life-skills development, education and career/job assistance. There's also the Men's Annex, which opened in 2014 and adds 78 more beds for the Regeneration Program.

In addition, there's the Center for Women and Children. The 40-bed facility houses single women as well as women with young children. The goal is to equip these women with the tools to be successful, and that includes coping/parenting classes, computer education and anger management, as needed.

There's also a non-residential Miami Community Activity Center, which opened in 2001 and provides preventative programs for at-risk children and youth in the adjoining neighborhood. Nearly 100 children are served with an after-school program that runs throughout the school year.

In the summer, the CAC holds a camp that provides daily activities for kids who otherwise would be left at home unattended. The activities include sports, tutoring, swimming lessons, arts and crafts and special field trips. Various volunteer groups provide specialized events for the children.

The CAC has been so successful that in 2015 it opened CARE Elementary School (operating under a separate 501c3), which serves kindergarten through the sixth grade.

As the Miami Rescue Mission continues to grow, its positive impact multiplies.

For example, the mission has 11 multiplex homes in Miami-Dade and Broward counties. Those structures house about 60 men, women and children who have successfully graduated various programs. Graduates pay monthly fees and are afforded continued aftercare. The goal is for graduates to continue their independence in safe and affordable housing.

Additionally, on a daily basis, the mission provides meals, showers and changes of clothing for 300 to 600 needy people, most of whom are unemployed or underemployed.

Four "street outreach" events are held annually in an effort to serve those who are hungry, needy and/or are experiencing homelessness. Thousands of people have attended these outreaches, and many of them have made the decision to come in off the street and into one of the mission's life-changing programs.

Here are some statistics to help explain what the Miami Rescue Mission accomplishes in a year:

= One million meals served to the hungry;

= 400,000 nights of emergency shelter;

= 250,000 hours of education, life skills and job training;

= 190,000 pieces of clothing given to those in need;

= 95,000 hours of volunteer time to the ministry;

= 78,000 hours given to kids in the mission's after-school program;

= 1,500 families helped with food, furnishings and toys.

One tangible and quite amazing number to come out of all this is that hundreds of graduates of the centers find employment and affordable housing each year.

Lastly, health care is a huge component to what the Miami Rescue Mission does for the community.

The dream of opening a clinic to meet the needs of the men, women and children in the mission's residential program became a reality in 2009 in Miami. One year later, the mission opened a health clinic in Hollywood.

These clinics were opened in a partnership with Miami Dade College's Medical Campus and with the added collaboration and assistance from the University of Miami, Florida International

University, Barry University, Nova Southeastern University, Broward College, Ross University, Baptist Health, Boston Scientific Foundation, the Michael Capponi Group and others.

Currently, there are three locations (Miami, Hollywood and Doral) for the health clinic. Each clinic operates with a paid staff and volunteer interns and physicians from various teaching colleges in the community.

The Miami Rescue Mission is now known as The Caring Place. The vision is simply this: "No One Is Homeless."

Celebrating their 100th-year anniversary in 2022, The Caring Place is on a great path all the way through and into the next century. The mission is expanding its footprint to help even more people, providing more permanent housing for the future.

It is a miracle in the making,

Indeed, the best is yet to come.

Afterword

by Reverend Ronald Brummitt

There were three things I desperately wanted growing up: love, acceptance and approval. They were, however, in short supply. While most kids couldn't wait to get home after school, I feared it. I never knew what I would come home to and if I were going to be safe.

My experiences growing up led me on a path that many children coming from rough family backgrounds go on.

Alcohol and drugs change people. My father was actually a really nice guy – just not when he was drinking. And he was drinking most of the time.

Eventually, I filled the missing parts of me with alcohol and drugs just like my folks. By the time I reached adulthood, I was homeless and an addict. It was a life I vowed I would never have.

Had I not found a small slant of light in my journey, I wouldn't be leading the Miami Rescue Mission. I wouldn't be doing anything; I would be dead. This I know for a fact. My spiral downward was strong and fierce. But I always believed, even in the worst of times, that God puts your feet where they need to be. On a cold Miami night, he did that for me. I found the light I needed. It came from the Miami Rescue Mission and Dr. Jacobs' kind hand on my shoulder.

My hope is that this book has inspired you with real stories of people who have overcome great adversity with even greater faith and support from the Miami Rescue Mission now known as The Caring Place. As the mission celebrates 100 years, we owe it to all those who came before us and all those who follow in our footsteps to share our hearts and our message.

While we are proud to be one of the largest social agencies in the country, we are also humbled that our ministry has the privilege of helping thousands of people each year. Changing one life at a time, that's what it's all about, isn't it? Whether you have sent up a prayer for those less fortunate, made in-kind donations, supported our cause financially or even with a kind word, we thank you. You have helped us make miracles happen at the Miami Rescue Mission.

Here's one thing I would like to leave you with from my very long and wonderful journey (yes, even the rough parts taught me great things): You don't have to be homeless to feel the need to be changed. The Miami Rescue Mission is the story of a ministry. For many, it continues to be a story of hope.

And hope is a story that belongs to all of us.

About the Author

Walter Villa was born in New York City and raised in Miami by wonderful Cuban-born parents.

Villa started his career in earnest as a sports editor for The Miami Herald. Following that, he served as deputy sports editor for The Pittsburgh Tribune-Review.

Since then, Villa has enjoyed a second career as a writer. He has been published by The New York Times, USA Today, The Miami Herald, The Boston Globe, The Los Angeles Times, Baseball America, Sports Illustrated.com, The Sporting News, D1 Baseball.com and many more.

The Miracle Mission is his first book.

His second book, Beyond Haiku: Pilot Stories, is coming soon.